13   (8/14)   14634

DISCOVER YOUR PSYC

In the same series

DISCOVER ASTRAL PROJECTION
J. H. Brennan
DISCOVER ASTROLOGY
Cordelia Mansall
DISCOVER CRYSTALS
Ursula Markham
DISCOVER DREAMS
Nerys Dee
DISCOVER GRAPHOLOGY
Margaret Gullan-Whur
DISCOVER NUMEROLOGY
Julia Line
DISCOVER PALMISTRY
Nathaniel Altman
DISCOVER RUNES
Tony Willis
DISCOVER TAROT
Emily Peach

DISCOVER YOUR PSYCHIC POWERS

RODNEY DAVIES

Aquarian/Thorsons
An Imprint of HarperCollins*Publishers*

The Aquarian Press
An Imprint of HarperCollins*Publishers*
77–85 Fulham Palace Road,
Hammersmith, London W6 8JB

Published by The Aquarian Press as *The ESP Workbook* 1987
This edition, revised and reset, 1992
1 3 5 7 9 10 8 6 4 2

© Rodney Davies 1987, 1992

Rodney Davies asserts the moral right to
be identified as the author of this work.
All the figures are drawn by the author.

A catalogue record for this book
is available from the British Library

ISBN 1 85538 139 7

Typeset by Harper Phototypesetters Limited,
Northampton, England
Printed in Great Britain by
Woolnough Bookbinding Limited,
Irthlingborough, Northamptonshire

All rights reserved. No part of this publication may be
reproduced, stored in a retrieval system, or transmitted,
in any form or by any means, electronic, mechanical,
photocopying, recording or otherwise, without the prior
permission of the publishers.

To my Mother, Peggy and Ken,
and to my late wife Maureen.

A deep below the deep,
And a height beyond the height!
Our hearing is not hearing,
And our seeing is not sight.

Alfred Tennyson

Contents

	Introduction	9
1.	Telepathy	17
2.	Mind Control	30
3.	Clairvoyance	34
4.	Dowsing	51
5.	Psychometry	57
6.	Precognition	66
7.	Scrying and Hypnotism	86
8.	The Oracles	93
9.	Psychokinesis	102
10.	Levitation	115
11.	Animal ESP	122
12.	Astral Projection	128
13.	Life After Death	141
14.	Further Communication	147
	Epilogue	156
	Index	157

Introduction

The object of this book is to show you how to explore and develop those powers of the human organism that come under the general heading of extra-sensory perception, or ESP, as opposed to those provided by the five ordinary senses of sight, hearing, taste, touch and smell. In fact, our ESP abilities are sometimes referred to as our 'sixth sense', although their diverse nature perhaps makes this too narrow a label. And because they are not wholly sensory in function, the term 'psi abilities' is often used instead of ESP.

By no means everybody is convinced that we possess extra-sensory perception, and there are many who believe that it is either illusory or is produced, where demonstrated, by trickery. There are of course professional mentalists or 'mind readers' who employ deception and certain well-practised techniques to achieve their ends, but this does not mean that extra-sensory perception is a sham, any more than the discovery of a forged masterpiece invalidates other works by the artist in question.

Indeed, there is now sufficient evidence of both an anecdotal and experimental nature to persuade all but the most prejudiced materialist that extra-sensory abilities are possessed in some degree by everyone, yourself included. And because it is not my intention to argue what is an already well-proven case, it is assumed that you, the reader, believe in ESP and wish to discover more about it and its applications, the talents of its stars, and the contributions of its investigators.

Hence we shall be examining *telepathy, clairvoyance, precognition* and *retrocognition*, and also the practical use of these abilities in *dowsing, psychometry* and *crystal-gazing*, and their manifestation in *dreams*. We shall likewise consider the mind's ability to influence objects at a distance, which is known as *psychokinesis*. Lastly, we shall examine *out-of-the-body-experiences*, and discuss how these support the notion that there is a *life after death*.

At present no one has a clear idea of how extra-sensory perception occurs because there are no special sense organs that can account for it, despite claims that the pineal gland or 'third eye' is the centre of ESP activity. This probably means that extra-sensory perception is a function of the mind itself, which is somehow able either to send or acquire information and to impress its will upon the environment directly. This ability is made even more enigmatic by the fact that it is not diminished by distance or impeded by it, as our other senses are, nor is it confined to the present moment but can range both forwards and backwards in time.

So described, extra-sensory perception seems to be an almost magical ability, one belonging more to the world of myth and faery than to everyday reality. And this is why many scientists, whose forebears waged a long battle against ignorance and superstition in the eighteenth and nineteenth centuries, are hostile to the very idea of ESP, or who, at best, prefer to ignore it, despite the positive results obtained by those few who have experimentally investigated it.

And yet support for the possibility of ESP does come from the discoveries of quantum physicists, who work at the cutting edge of science. They have introduced such concepts as relativity, action-at-a-glance, anti-matter, black holes and parallel universes to both their colleagues and to the general public, and these are equally as enigmatic and as seemingly unlikely, in terms of Newtonian physics, as ESP.

Physicists now know that electrons can individually occupy two places at the same time, that their rate of spin can be altered by other electrons having their rotation rate either speeded up or slowed down, and that they can apparently move forwards, and possibly backwards, in time. And while such paradoxical behaviour by sub-atomic particles does not explain how the mind senses or directly affects external objects, it gives credence to the idea of it functioning in this way.

For we live in a strange and very complex universe, wherein things are not as they seem and whose mysteries may never be fully understood. And because every door that science opens merely exposes more doors, our quest for 'ultimate truth' may well be as vain as looking for the pot of gold at the end of a rainbow.

Indeed, what we commonly call reality is an illusion created by our brains. Our sense organs are only activated by certain types of information – by particular wavelengths of light and by vibrations in the air, for example – and the signals they send to the brain are then transformed into a rough three-dimensional representation of what lies around us, whose accuracy is sufficient to allow us to survive and reproduce.

But even the white pages of this book and the black type that crosses them have no objective colour reality. The pages are white and the type is black only because your brain gives them those shades in the light conditions pertaining at this instant. And does your room seem quiet, except perhaps for the ticking of the clock? It may seem that way, but it is of course filled with radio and television signals that you cannot yourself detect, although if these are changed into sound and light waves by the right electronic equipment, you would not doubt their presence. And do you and the chair upon which you sit feel solid? That too is an illusion, for both you and it are predominantly empty space, through which various types of electromagnetic radiation and sub-atomic particles pass without hindrance, and without disturbing the atoms that give it the impression of substance. Hence we are all shadows in a world of shadows, and it is only our brains that give form to such formlessness.

Yet the average scientist still insists on regarding nature as a solid actuality that operates according to certain well-defined laws, all of which are capable of discovery given sufficient funds and the right experimental method.

'One might have expected,' said the psychic researcher G. N. M. Tyrrel, 'that to a man endowed with true scientific curiosity, the merest hint of telepathy would act like the scent of battle to a war-horse. But the scientist does not behave in the least like a war-horse. He behaves much more like a mule: neither pushing nor pulling will move him. When the real test comes, he proves himself to be an *a priori* theorist at heart.'

This is why, should you have some doubts about the reality of extra-sensory perception, you will find the 'do-it-yourself' experiments outlined in this book useful. With luck, they will convince you that you do have extra-sensory capabilities.

With luck? Yes, because our psychic abilities do not function as mechanically as our other sense organs. They are subject to our moods, to the conditions pertaining at the time, and to the varying receptivity of our brains. Hence our extra-sensory perceptivity rises and falls, rather like our spirits, which is why many ESP experiments give ambiguous results.

One big difficulty in evaluating ESP phenomena is deciding whether or not they were caused by chance. After all, if I suddenly find myself thinking about a friend whom I haven't seen or contacted for some time, who then, much to my surprise, telephones me, is that a chance happening or is it a demonstration of ESP? Simple chance could account for it, naturally enough, and we would have to weigh the odds for such a coincidence taking place very carefully. To do this we would want to know if my friend in normal circumstances telephones me often or not, and how long the 'some time' is since he last telephoned. Was it days, weeks, months or years? And we would likewise want to know if I had any reason for expecting him to telephone, which might make the fact of him telephoning while I was thinking about him more likely.

But even if such considerations indicated that the likelihood of him telephoning at that moment was extremely small – if, for example, the chance of it happening was one in a million – this still would not prove that one or other of us had telepathically received the other's thoughts, even though I myself might believe that it did.

In actual fact something very similar happened to me in 1979, although the incident had a rather interesting twist to it. It may remind you of similar occurrences in your life.

On 15 November of that year I drove from Glastonbury in Somerset, where I had been staying, to Hastings, to visit my aunt. Realizing that my journey would take me very close to Chandlers Ford in Hampshire, I considered stopping to visit my old schoolfriend Peter B., who lives there. I had last seen Peter on 15 March 1977 – some two and a half years before – and had neither written to nor telephoned him during that time. I felt guilty about not keeping in touch, and it was this sense of guilt, plus my dislike of turning up unannounced, allied with my belief that he would not be at home anyway (it was a weekday), that made me decide, as I neared Chandlers Ford, to keep going.

When I arrived at Hastings, I was annoyed with myself for not at least stopping and trying his doorbell; had there been no reply I could have left a note explaining that I had just passed through Chandlers Ford and hoped to see him again some time in the not-too-distant future, etc. But the opportunity had gone and there was nothing I could do about it.

I stayed at Hastings until 20 November, when I drove home to London. I arrived back at 7 p.m. and was sitting down to enjoy a cup of tea about one hour later when the telephone rang – and lo and behold the caller turned out to be Peter B., who quickly explained that he was telephoning to invite me down to Chandlers Ford to stay with him and his wife!

In the event, Peter's timing was spot on. Had he telephoned only two hours earlier he would not have found me at home. Thus it appeared to me that he had not only picked up my thoughts about him, but had somehow sensed when would be the right time to telephone. All in all, it was apparently a quite startling example of extra-sensory perception.

Two months later a similar happening took place. This concerned Raymond B., who edited a horoscope magazine in Montreal, Canada, for which I was then doing some regular work. Because of the distance involved, Ray rarely telephoned; once, or at the most, twice a year, according to the need, was his maximum. He wrote somewhat more often, and I had received a letter from him in October 1979, in which he gave me his new address. This letter, once read, had been put away and forgotten about.

On the evening of 21 January 1980, I decided to resume work on a novel I had begun the previous spring. I took the manuscript out from the drawer where it was kept, and underneath it I found Ray's letter. I read it through again and immediately began wondering if I had made a note of his new address. I checked my address book, discovered that I had not, and took it down. Then I went into my office to work – and ten minutes later Ray telephoned me from Montreal. There was no problem, he told me, he just wanted to call and find out how I was. Now was that simple coincidence, or had he somehow, at a distance of about three thousand miles, picked up my thoughts and been prompted by them to telephone me? Ray himself could not answer that, because all he was aware of was a sudden wish to telephone me, which he then did.

But that was not the only possible paranormal experience that happened to me on 21 January 1980. I also had what I believe to be a precognitive insight, one that is worth mentioning because it demonstrates the relative triviality of such experiences, and also the way in which the mind often views the future in a crab-wise fashion.

Late on that Monday afternoon, while out for a drive, I suddenly started thinking about the 'Milky Bar Kid' advertisement that had been on television some years previously, and I wondered what had become of the boy who played him. I then recalled seeing him featured in a 'Where Are They Now?' programme that had been broadcast about a year before. But I was at a loss to know why his whereabouts should be of interest to me.

Downfall of the Milky Bar Kid

Daily Mail Reporter

TO his school pals, he was just like the Milky Bar Kid in the TV adverts.

The boy with the blazer pockets full of chocolate was always handing out goodies to friends—until his teachers found out.

They became suspicious and called police to the school near Bristol.

That wiped the smile off the chocolate - smeared f a c e s around the other Milky Bar Kid.

'Turn out your pockets,' he was told. And out came a wad of £500.

Lavished

'I took it from a case under my dad's bed,' explained the Kid.

Police told the boy's father what had happened . . . and searched the house. There, was £58,000 in notes in the case under the bed.

The father said he had been given the money by three East London businessmen to help them in a venture.

Flying Squad detectives interviewed the three men, a father and his two sons, at Walthamstow police station. They were allowed home after questioning.

A police spokesman said : 'We wanted to know how such a large sum in cash had been obtained.

'The lad appears to have taken about £1,000 in all from the case and lavished gifts on friends.'

Figure 1: Cutting from the *Daily Mail*

The reason why I had thought about the Milky Bar Kid became plain the very next morning when, leafing through the *Daily Mail*, my eye was suddenly caught by a page three headline, which read 'Downfall of the Milky Bar Kid'. The article beneath it was not about the Milky Bar Kid of whom I had been thinking, but concerned a schoolboy who had stolen some money from the case-full he had found under his father's bed. He had used this to buy chocolate, which he had then lavished upon his friends, so that 'to his school pals, he was just like the Milky Bar Kid in the TV adverts'.

Once again, simple coincidence could account for this. With a readership of about two million, it is quite likely that someone among that number might think about the subject of an article featured in the *Daily Mail* the day before it appeared, even though the piece was an unusual, one-off insert, and I could have been that person.

It is also possible, however, that I had somehow obtained a precognitive glimpse at the following morning's newspaper, which had enabled me to 'catch sight' of the headline in question and which had started me off thinking about the Milky Bar Kid of television fame. If so, it demonstrates that precognitive experiences are not necessarily appreciated for what they are. During my drive I had not thought to myself 'I'm going to see an article headed "Downfall of the Milky Bar Kid" in tomorrow's *Daily Mail*.' Rather, as I indicated above, I had glimpsed a future headline and this had set in motion a train of thought that I found puzzling.

I have mentioned these three occurrences because they all happened within a short period of time, two in fact taking place on the same day, which further suggests that something other than chance was at work, and because they are probably similar to the sort of experience that you have had or will have.

That I am able to write about them and the other experiences I recount later on, is because I made a note of them at the time. And you should do the same. In this way you will be able to acquire a record of possible paranormal happenings, that you will be able to refer to and quote with accuracy at a later date. This is particularly important where the events themselves are of little importance, as otherwise they will be quickly forgotten. I am quite sure I would have long forgotten about Peter and Ray telephoning when they did, and about the Milky Bar Kid episode, had I not jotted down the details, clipped out the newspaper article, and also kept Ray's letter.

Where possible you should likewise tell what you have felt, dreamed or experienced to at least one other person, who will, if necessary, be able to substantiate what you say. Witnesses are most easily found where presentiments are concerned, because there is usually a delay in time between the feeling that something is going to happen or the dream about it, and the actual event. But it is much more difficult obtaining witnesses for possible telepathic or clairvoyant experiences, as this would mean having to constantly inform someone of our thoughts.

In Britain, the Society for Psychical Research is always interested in hearing about witnessed first-hand accounts of paranormal happenings, while the British Premonitions Bureau, formed after the Aberfan tragedy in 1966, welcomes receiving reports of premonitions, because its staff believe that these could be used to save lives. And there are similar organizations in other countries, most particularly in the USA.

However, I must add that information gained by extra-sensory perception is not always immediately recognized as such, while conscious expectations or simple chance happenings can sometimes be mistaken for ESP. Thus greater awareness and caution is needed to ensure that the wheat is kept separate from the chaff. And contrary to popular belief, most

ESP experiences do not relate to dramatic events, but to ordinary, everyday occurrences, which is why they are so often missed or overlooked.

So do keep a record of your experiences, try to obtain one or more witnesses of them, and always expect the unexpected.

Chapter 1
Telepathy

Telepathy ('far-feeling') is the direct communication, voluntary or involuntary, of one mind with another. Thus described, it is usual to imagine that the thoughts of one person (the 'agent') are somehow sent or beamed to the conscious mind of another (the 'percipient'), rather like radio or television signals travelling from the transmitting station to the appropriate aerial. Indeed, this notion of 'thought transmission' is implied by the title of Upton Sinclair's celebrated book on the subject: *Mental Radio, Does It Work and How?* (1929).

Such an idea is, however, almost certainly wrong. All known information signals, like light, sound waves, electromagnetic radiation, etc., dissipate with distance, are impeded by physical barriers, and take time to travel from A to B. But telepathic communication is not so affected: it can bridge vast distances without losing its force, it is unimpeded by any known physical barrier, and it is instantaneous. Hence it cannot be accounted for by the movement of some mysterious energy, as this would certainly be subjected to the same hindrances as other signals. Instead, it seems likely that telepathy is the synchronous growth of the same idea or set of ideas in two minds at the same time. One of these minds may well be the agent or originator, the other the percipient or receiver, but to all intents and purposes each mind generates the same thought or thoughts independently of the other. Nothing, therefore, travels between them.

Such simultaneous generation is quite unknown in the physical world, which is why we have difficulty in comprehending it. But the realm of the mind is non-physical, wherein the same laws do not apply. This is why psychic powers have been called supernatural, and why they are sometimes still viewed with suspicion and fear. Yet though poorly understood and intermittent in operation, such 'mind powers' and the way in which they function are entirely natural, and it is to be hoped that they will one day attract the scientific attention that they so richly deserve.

Telepathy is not a mental capacity that has been recently discovered or wondered about, even though it is only during the last hundred years that it has been experimentally investigated. Mankind's recognition of it is extremely ancient, although its occurrence was usually ascribed to a spirit or a god, who was believed to have 'passed on' the thoughts of person A to person B. Indeed, our telepathic, clairvoyant and precognitive abilities appear to have atrophied in modern times, when we have become cut off from the rhythms of nature, from quietness and inner peace, and from an acceptance of the possibility of such things, all of which heighten extra-sensory perception. The members of primitive tribes often possess quite remarkable powers in this respect, to the extent of knowing what a distant tribesman is doing, the whereabouts of water, game and other non-observable necessities, and the outcome of a particular course of action; talents that are generally greatly reduced or lost completely when they are 'civilized'. In her book *Across Lapland*, Olive Chapman observes: 'Many of the people undoubtedly possessed what today would be called psychic powers, for they have had frequent knowledge of events that were happening at a distance . . . (this) was sternly denounced by the missionary, Laestadius, and his followers, who declared it to be of the Devil, and as such to be rigorously suppressed.'

It is for this reason that you should not expect to achieve immediate success when you test your own powers of extra-sensory perception. For they may, like Sleeping Beauty, need to be woken up and then gently encouraged to grow and bloom. Most people, however, can recall one or more incidents in their lives when they somehow 'knew' what was happening or what was going to happen, despite the fact that they could not have gained this knowledge by normal sensory means. You may well have had such experiences. If so, your ESP abilities are still functioning, if only at a low level.

But quite often we ignore those impressions that we do get, usually because they are at variance with what we want to happen. Thus having made an appointment with a friend, for example, you may suddenly think to yourself, 'Oh, she's not going to be there', which you immediately contradict by saying 'Of course she is.' So you set off to keep the appointment, not wanting to believe that your friend won't be there, because you are looking forward to seeing her again and because you have no confidence in your 'silly' feelings, only to find that your friend does not turn up and that your journey is wasted. You then kick yourself for not believing what you felt, even though you knew you were not prepared to risk being wrong.

Similarly, we often mistake ideas that have been generated in another person's mind for our own. Thus I may think to myself 'I must write to Iola tonight' and believe this to be a consciously-made decision, whereas Iola might have previously thought to herself 'I wish Rodney would write to me', which telepathically produced my thought. I will have had no indication that any telepathic communication took place, as neither will Iola, who will simply be pleasantly surprised when my letter arrives. This is surely what happened with Peter B. and Raymond B., whose decisions to telephone me followed on from my thoughts about them.

Telepathy usually occurs between people who know each other, and most often between those who are emotionally involved, such as family members, friends and lovers. It rarely takes place between strangers, which is why rape or murder victims are seldom psychically apprised of their assailant's intentions and so warned of the attack. Also, what sense of disquiet they may feel is often consciously discounted.

Telepathic communication, perhaps hardly surprisingly, is strongest between mother and child, and there are many accounts of a mother sensing when something untoward is happening to her offspring. The following example of such communication, quoted by Dr William Heaps in his book *Psychic Phenomena*, happened to a woman friend of his living in Connecticut, USA.

'In many suburban areas,' she said, 'friends and neighbours having swimming pools share them with other families lacking them. These are generally scheduled on warm summer days. One day I dropped off my young son to enjoy a swim. I was to call for him after I had completed shopping and a number of errands. Within an hour, while in a supermarket I felt that he was in danger. I even saw him on the bottom of the pool in the deep end. So strong was this feeling that I left the supermarket immediately . . . The pool was half a mile away and I broke the speed laws and even ran through stop lights getting there. I rushed to the poolside, and failed to see my son in the water or near it. The children told me they had not seen him for some time, and I circled the pool to the deep end. He was lying on the bottom! Two of the older boys dived in and brought him out. He was not breathing and had turned purple. Fortunately . . . after what seemed an interminable time, Jimmy was finally revived.'

This woman's telepathic awareness of her son's difficulties in the swimming pool enabled her to save his life, and a great many other mothers – and fathers, too – have experienced similar telepathic communication with their children, even though this may not have been brought about by so dramatic a happening.

The example points up another factor, other than that of the close relationship between the two people involved, in telepathic communication – the strength of feeling of the percipient matches that of the agent. The son's fear and panic not only gave rise to a sense 'that he was in danger' in the mother, but gave her a vision that he was 'on the bottom of the pool in the deep end'. Others have reported hearing the voice of the person in distress or of seeing him or her apparently appear before them. But when the incident is painful, yet not life threatening, such visionary experiences seldom occur.

'We were at a football game in Berkeley,' a young mother told the psychic researcher Ian Stevenson. 'My husband got up suddenly in the middle of the game and said we must go home as our son had been hurt. When we arrived home our son had shot a (steel pellet) into his thumb and we had to take him to a doctor to have it removed.'

Thus a psychic shout registers far more forcibly than a psychic whisper, and is therefore more likely to be recognized for what it is. And likewise, the percipient is better able to sense the thoughts of another if he or she is in a calm and relaxed state of mind.

Telepathic communication does not only alter the mental condition of the percipient; it may also be physically felt. This accounts for the widely-held belief that when our ears start to burn for no apparent reason, it indicates that someone is talking about us. In fact I recommend that when this next happens to you, you make a note of the time and date and also try to 'tune in' to whoever might be thinking or talking about you. If you get an idea of who it is and what they are thinking or saying, ask the person concerned if your feelings were right. And even if you cannot sense who the person is, enquire amongst your family and friends if any were thinking or talking about you. You will probably be very surprised at the result.

Experiments involving telepathy were begun about one hundred years ago and the form that many of them took was similar to that employed by Gilbert Murray (1866-1957), Regius Professor of Greek at the University of Oxford, which he described in his Presidential address to the Society of Psychical Research in 1915.

'I go out of the parlour and of course out of earshot of my family and friends there. Someone in the room, generally my eldest daughter Rosalind, thinks of a scene or incident or anything she likes, and says it aloud. It is written down and I am called into the room. I come in, usually take my daughter's hand, and then, if I have luck, describe in detail what she has thought of. However, the least disturbance of our customary method – change of time, the presence of strangers, and especially noise of any kind – is apt to make things go wrong.'

For instance, when 'that funny old Irishman called Dr Hunt in the hotel in Jamaica' was chosen as the subject, Murray was able to say: 'It's – it must (have) something to do with Jamaica. I can't get it clear. I felt as if it were a drunken Irish doctor talking with a brogue.' Out of the first five hundred of these trials that Murray took part in, it was estimated that one-third of his responses were correct and about thirty per cent were partially correct, a remarkably high score. And although such parlour game tests have been criticized by later researchers as being too difficult to evaluate statistically, it is evident that the emotional closeness of the participants, and their interest and enjoyment in the proceedings, contributed to Murray's high rate of success.

Indeed, you might like to test your own ESP abilities in the same way. I say 'ESP abilities' rather than 'telepathic abilities', because it now seems clear that Murray obtained at least part of his answers by clairvoyance. Hence, because it is impossible to distinguish what is gained by telepathy and what by clairvoyance, it is safest to regard Murray's parlour game as a test of General ESP (or GESP).

As we have already seen, telepathy is direct mind-to-mind communication, whereas clairvoyance is the ability of one mind to obtain information about distant events directly. This suggests that while Murray sat in the parlour he could have clairvoyantly 'listened in' to what was being decided upon in the other room; or he could have similarly 'read' what was written down; or he might have 'picked up' the subject matter of the experiment in such a way from his daughter, whose hand he held. And he might also, of course, have received the information telepathically.

Because any information gained from a group, which has to discuss what it is going to 'send' telepathically before it does so, may be divined clairvoyantly, it is only possible to perform a true test of telepathy when just two people are involved, the agent and the percipient. The agent mentally decides what he is going to 'send' and does not write this down until the percipient (or percipients) has made a note of his impressions. Then both writings are compared and the amount of agreement or disagreement is recorded. In this way any correct information could only have been obtained by telepathy, always providing that the subject was not something that could have been guessed or consciously inferred.

Should you try Murray's parlour game or a one-to-one telepathy test, it is important to make sure that the percipient (who could be either yourself or one of the other people) is in a relaxed state of mind. The subject chosen can be as simple as someone's name (e.g. 'Mary Smith'), or that of an object (e.g. 'a hammer') or as complex as 'that funny old Irishman called Dr Hunt in the hotel in Jamaica'. The recipient may obtain an exact image of the subject, or he may pick up associated words and ideas. For example, if the subject is 'a hammer', he may report that he gained a sense of 'something being struck' or 'the act of striking', or see an image of 'a nail or nails', or 'a mallet' or perhaps 'a pickaxe'. None of these are spot on, but they are close enough to the actual subject to suggest that telepathy has occurred.

The Soviet Union's most sensitive telepathic percipient, Karl Nikolayev, who has participated in several long-distance telepathy experiments with agent Yuri Kemensky, such as that conducted in 1966 between Moscow and Novosibirsk, has said this about his mental impressions when receiving:

'I see before my inner eye something like the screen of a small TV set. On it appears, very faintly at first, the outline of the object, as if the TV set has not been tuned in too sharply. Then the picture travels into my hand. I feel as though I can touch it to determine its shape and size, and the temperature of its surface. The longer I am touching it, the clearer is the image on this inner TV screen.'

However, the experiments of those individuals like Gilbert Murray and Upton Sinclair – the latter 'sent' telepathic images of pictures he had drawn to his wife Craig, who reproduced 65 (23 per cent) of the 290 drawings with complete success and 155 (53 per cent) with partial success – were criticized by scientists because they were not conducted under properly controlled and supervised conditions, and because it was

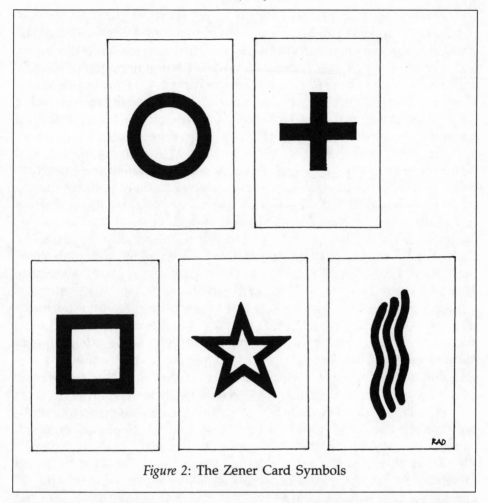

Figure 2: The Zener Card Symbols

impossible to estimate the chance-factor involved. And as I have already remarked, the positive results obtained, while supposedly acquired by telepathy, could have been produced by clairvoyance.

The realization that ESP experimentation needed to be carried out in the prescribed scientific manner if it was to be at all convincing led to a more formal approach being taken by Dr Joseph Banks Rhine (1895-1980) at Duke University, North Carolina.

Dr Rhine had trained originally as a botanist, but an interest in psychical research and in spiritualism prompted him to enter into correspondence with Professor William McDougall, the head of the Psychology Department at Harvard University, who had publicly stated that he thought extra-sensory perception should be actively investigated in universities. Their mutual interest in extra-sensory perception eventually led to McDougall offering Rhine a research post at Harvard, which he accepted. Then when McDougall moved to Duke University in 1927, Rhine went with him, and the two men founded the Parapsychological Laboratory, where Rhine's important ESP experiments were carried out.

Rhine conducted his research into telepathy using students and members of his own staff as subjects, rather than individuals known to be psychic, and the experiments were designed so that the chance factor could easily be calculated. This work took an important step forward when one of his team, Dr Karl Zener, invented a deck of special cards for this purpose, and which have since been extensively used in ESP experiments. Each white Zener card bears one of five basic symbols coloured black, these being a star, a cross, a circle, a square and three wavy lines (see Figure 2), and as there are twenty-five cards in the deck, so each symbol is represented five times. This means that in any card guessing experiment there is a one-in-five chance of a specific symbol turning up, thus for a subject working his way through the whole deck while attempting to identify each symbol by extra-sensory perception, chance alone would give him or her five correct guesses. Scores higher than that represent a positive deviation, and scores below that a negative deviation.

If you either buy yourself a deck of Zener cards or make one by reproducing the symbols shown on twenty-five pieces of card, you can carry out your own experiments similar to the early ones done by Dr Rhine. Let us, for example, imagine that you are going to act as the agent or sender, while your partner is the percipient. Here is what you do: sit apart from your partner, who should not of course be able to see the card faces, and who should be supplied with a pad upon which he can record his guesses. Then shuffle the cards well and place them face downwards in front of you. When the percipient indicates that he is ready to proceed, take up the top card and look at it, and try to telepathically 'send' its symbol to him. Once he has recorded his guess, place that card face down on the table to start another pile, then take up the next card and repeat the process. Continue until you have worked your way right through the deck. Next, check his guesses by calling out the card symbols in the order they appeared and have him tick off those he guessed correctly or, if you doubt his integrity, do it yourself.

Now I have said that chance alone should give your partner a correct score of five. But as you can appreciate, chance could result in higher scores, although the odds against this happening rise dramatically with each correct guess above five. Thus while a score of seven correct guesses represents odds of 20 to 1 against chance, this rises to 250 to 1 against chance if eight guesses prove correct. Odds of 20 to 1 against chance form what is known as the *point of significance* in scientific research, and results better than that are called *significant* – or, where we are concerned, demonstrative of extra-sensory perception. Yet you should not base your conclusions on one trial, but on several, as the correct score average of several trials is more accurate statistically than the result furnished by one trial. For example, suppose you do ten trials with the Zener cards and the percipient makes seventy-five correct guesses or 'hits' instead of the fifty suggested by chance, because this represents odds against chance of about 250 to 1, it strongly indicates that extra-sensory perception has taken place.

You may have noticed that I wrote 'extra-sensory perception' twice in the above paragraph, rather than telepathy – or you may have realized that the Zener card experiment as I described it could also be testing the percipient's clairvoyant ability. This was also appreciated by Dr Rhine, who after some twenty years of experimentation wrote:

'It now seems doubtful whether they (i.e. telepathy and clairvoyance) are two different processes at all . . . even though telepathy is both more popular, more familiar, and more readily acceptable even to the general scientist, it has proved a much more difficult phenomenon to investigate and isolate from clairvoyance experimentally.'

If you wish to undertake an experiment using the Zener cards that does test for telepathy and not clairvoyance, you will not be able to use the cards as such, because they might be 'seen' clairvoyantly, but only the symbols in the cards, which you will picture in your mind.

For this experiment, each of you will need a pad and a pencil. Both of you should write numbers from 1 to 25 down the side of the pad sheet, against which the percipient will record the symbol he receives and the agent the symbol he concentrates upon. Again, when the percipient signals that he is ready, you begin – only this time you think of one of the five Rhine symbols, you do not look at the cards at all. But you do not, however, record this until after the percipient has noted down his guess. Then, when you have done so, you can concentrate on another (or even the same) symbol. Do this twenty-five times to complete the trial.

However, there is one experimental rule that you must strictly adhere to, as otherwise the results will be too difficult to evaluate statistically: each symbol must only be thought of five times in all. So keep a careful check on those you have used as you go down the page.

Now although these card-guessing experiments might seem quite interesting to do, they quickly become tedious, which is why I suggest that you do not do too many at one session. And you should also take a break and relax between each trial.

One result of doing too many trials is a fall off in positive results as the experiment proceeds. This was first noticed in 1924 by Ina Jephson, a Member of Council of the Society of Psychical Research, who performed some telepathy experiments with playing cards. She carried out a total of six thousand trials using 240 subjects, who obtained an average score per trial of 13.03, as opposed to the average score of 11.14 that chance would have given. But while the overall result was positive, Miss Jephson discovered that they were greatest at first, but fell off later. This indicates that our extra-sensory capacities are diminished by boredom and repetition, hence there is little point in carrying on for too long as this is counter-productive.

It has also long been realized that percipients function best when they are mentally relaxed and physically at ease, whereas agents function most effectively when they have a real need to make telepathic contact, as when they are in a dangerous situation.

These two opposite mental and physical states are difficult to either expect of, or have reproduced in, those participating in laboratory experiments, which is perhaps why the results of many ESP experiments have been disappointing. In fact some experiments in telepathy, even those that have been done on a large scale, have only produced results at the chance level.

Another important factor, according to the parapsychologist Dr Gertrude Schmeidler, who conducted many ESP experiments after the Second World War, is the participants' attitude to extra-sensory perception. She found that those who believed in ESP tended to score positive results, while those that did not scored slightly less than chance. This in turn indicates that you are more likely to obtain positive results if you do your experiments with 'ESP believers' – and most particularly if these are family members or close friends.

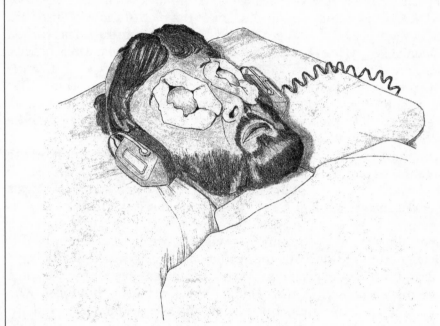

Figure 3: A subject inducing an altered state of consciousness by
means of the Ganzfeld technique

Yet while it is difficult to create the ideal mental state in the agent, there
are various ways in which the relaxed frame of mind necessary for
telepathic reception can be produced in the percipient. The simplest
method is for him to lie down in a quiet room for fifteen minutes before
the experiment proceeds.

Telepathic messages are readily 'picked up' by those who are asleep or
hypnotized – who are, in other words, in an altered state of
consciousness. One method of producing an altered state of consciousness
in a person who is awake was devised by the parapsychologist Charles
Honorton in the 1960s. This is the so-called Ganzfeld or 'whole field'
technique, whereby the mind of the percipient is presented with a set of
unstructured stimuli that contain no patterns and which, accordingly, do
not distract his attention or interfere with his extra-sensory receptivity.

The Ganzfeld subject lies comfortably on his back on a bed or couch,
and half a ping-pong ball is placed over each eye, standing on cotton wool

or Plasticine, which accords with the contours of the face and so stops direct light from entering under the rim of the ball. A red or white light source is then placed a few feet away. In this manner the subject, even if he opens his eyes, can only see a uniform field of soft light. Earphones are then fitted over his ears, and through these 'white noise' – a gentle swishing sound – is played. The subject is next allowed to relax for at least fifteen minutes, whereupon the telepathic transmissions can take place. The percipient can either record his responses on a tape recorder, or these are noted down by the experimenter.

Yet another factor that probably contributes to the success or otherwise of standard laboratory experiments is the concentrative powers of the agent or agents. As you will discover when you try to hold something as basic as the image of a Zener card symbol in your mind, this exercise is by no means easy to do. Images other than the one you wish to 'send' will keep slipping into your mind, as will all sorts of ideas and thoughts that have nothing to do with the matter in hand. Practice will help, of course, and you should get better at retaining images in your mind as time goes by, which should in turn lead to better results. Thus those who produce higher scores than the average, like Yuri Kemensky and his partner Karl Nikolayev, probably do so because the agent is able to hold a clear image in his consciousness, and the percipient can remove extraneous thoughts and ideas from his.

One way that has been employed of 'spicing up' the agent and, even more remarkably, the percipient, is to have the agent view visual material that is more interesting than simple shapes like the Zener symbols. This was first tried by Dr Don Donderi, Associate Professor of Psychology at McGill University, Montreal, in the early 1970s.

'We devised a more interesting method of testing,' he told me, 'hoping that the visual material we used – films – would prove more stimulating and lead to, perhaps, better results.'

Donderi and his former student Howard Eisenberg obtained seven short films from the National Film Board of Canada and edited each down to seven minutes in length. During the editing, the most strikingly visual part of the films was retained and the remainder discarded.

The researchers then advertized for volunteers on the McGill campus and drew a response from fifty-two men and women. Their ages ranged from fourteen to forty-four and about three-quarters were students. The volunteers were paired off and randomly assigned the role of agent and percipient. Each was given a searching personality test.

'On seven successive days, the sender of each pair was required to view each of the films in turn,' Donderi explained. 'While he or she did this, the receiver was relaxing in another room in a different part of the building. When the film had been screened, the sender was instructed to write a report of what he had seen and of his emotional responses to the material. While he did this, the receiver was simultaneously instructed to write a similar report, basing what he wrote on whatever telepathic information he might have picked up.'

The participants also had to complete a structured questionnaire and sort five photographs, one of which was a still from the film, into a descending order of pictorial relevance to the theme of the film. The reports, questionnaires and photos were then removed and independently evaluated for correspondences.

'When all the results had been analysed and matched against chance correspondences,' added Dondori, 'we found that the receivers were reporting information that could only have come to them by extra-sensory perception – by telepathy. In this we confirmed the results obtained by other researchers. But what we didn't manage to demonstrate was any relationship between telepathic ability and personality, which is something that other workers have shown.'

Dr Donderi also said that he was personally convinced that telepathy is a real, rather than an apparent, faculty of the human mind, although he had no idea how it occurs.

But while his method may well have had a stimulating effect on both the mind of the agent and the percipient, it is impossible to tell if the percipients obtained the information they acquired by telepathy or by clairvoyance, as both were possible under the experimental conditions employed.

Chapter 2
Mind Control

The telepathic interchange of information between minds can and does happen, and while the means by which it takes place is unknown, there is general agreement among parapsychologists that it is a reality. But if so, it naturally raises the question as to whether commands can be sent telepathically, thereby enabling the sender to control not only the recipient's thoughts and feelings but his behaviour as well.

The Soviet dictator Joseph Stalin wondered exactly the same thing when, during the last war, he watched a performance given by the celebrated mind reader or mentalist Wolf Messing. So impressed was Stalin by Messing's apparent ability both to read minds and to mentally direct the actions of others, that he devised a stringent experiment to test his powers.

Not long afterwards, Messing was collected from his apartment by two burly men, who took him to the Moscow Goss bank. They gave the startled mentalist an attaché case and told him to go into the bank and demand, by mental command alone, 100,000 roubles, an enormous sum of money, from the cashier. If successful, he was to bring the money out for them to witness.

But if such a demand would have daunted a lesser man, the great Wolf Messing rose to the occasion. He entered the bank.

'I walked up to the cashier, who was an elderly man, and gave him a blank piece of paper that I had torn from an old school notebook,' Messing later recalled. 'I then willed him to give me 100,000 roubles.'

The cashier carefully inspected the piece of paper, and then, evidently satisfied that it was a valid document authorizing payment, he went to the safe and counted out from it the 100,000 roubles. Messing hurriedly put the bundles of notes into his attaché case, thanked the cashier and

Figure 4: Wolf Messing

left the bank to rejoin Stalin's henchmen. They checked the money through to satisfy themselves that Messing had done as the dictator had ordered and then told him to return it.

The poor cashier stared at Messing in surprise as he handed back the money. His surprise turned to horror when he again examined what he had thought was an official cheque, only to find that it was a crumpled piece of blank paper. The shock was too much for his system and he collapsed, the victim of a heart attack.

Wolf Grigorievich Messing was born in Poland in 1891. An only son, he grew into a slightly-built, dark-haired, shy young man, who astounded his family and friends by seeming to know what they were going to say before they said it, by finding objects that they had hidden or lost, by following their unspoken mental commands and, perhaps most incredibly, by being able to telepathically direct their actions. Later on, he was to develop the ability of seeing into the future.

Capitalizing on these gifts, he became a professional 'mind-reader', thrilling and amazing audiences with his psychic virtuosity. Yet as he established a comfortable, middle-class life for himself, shadows were gathering elsewhere in Europe as the Nazis came to power in Germany.

Then, on 1 September 1939, the German army invaded Poland. It was an event that changed Messing's life. For eighteen months later, when the Nazis went on to invade the Soviet Union, he was rash enough to predict that they would be defeated by the Russians and that Adolf Hitler would die not long afterwards.

His arrest was ordered, obliging Messing to flee to the Soviet Union, where he was to spend the rest of his life.

For the remainder of the war and until his death in 1966, Messing worked for the State booking agency Goskonzert as a mentalist, travelling the length and breadth of the Soviet Union, putting on shows in villages, towns and cities, entertaining the public. It was a busy, exhausting life, and one that he came to hate, notwithstanding the fact that it brought him a pleasant three-room apartment in Moscow and a regular monthly salary.

It was during a performance in Moscow that Messing was seen by Joseph Stalin, who was enormously impressed by his act. He was even more impressed when Messing used his powers to withdraw the 100,000 roubles from the Goss bank. It was a success that led the Soviet leader to order one last, and seemingly impossible, test. Stalin told the psychic that he was to try and enter his country dacha and make his way to the room – Russia's holy of holies – where he worked. Taken aback, yet quietly confident, Messing said that he would do so if he could.

One afternoon a few days later, while Stalin was busy working on some State papers, Messing walked into the dacha without attracting any attention. In fact Stalin's personal bodyguard stood back respectfully as he walked down a hallway, past several rooms, to the open door of Stalin's study. The dictator stared up at him in astonishment as he entered. Messing saluted him and smiled. He had achieved the impossible!

But how, Stalin wanted to know, had he done it?

'I mentally suggested to the guards and everyone else I met, "I am Beria, I am Beria",' Messing explained. Thus by mental command alone (for Messing was physically quite different from the stout Beria) he had turned himself into the head of Stalin's feared secret police, who frequently visited the dacha.

It was at about this time that Messing made one of his most remarkable predictions. During a performance in Novosibirsk on 7 March 1944, he publicly announced that the war would end on 9 May 1945, a prediction that turned out to be absolutely correct.

When asked shortly before his death how he foresaw the future, Messing replied:

'By straining my will-power, I suddenly see the culminating result of a stream of events. I call it "direct knowledge". I don't see anything mystical about it. The future shapes itself from the past and the present, and there are certain models or bonds between them. Understanding the mechanism of this direct knowledge is at present inaccessible to us, because our ideas of the essence of time, of its ties with space, with the past, present, and future are as yet indefinite.'

Messing's direct knowledge of the future saved his life on at least one occasion. This happened in 1948 on the day that he arrived in the southern capital of Ashkhabad, where he was booked to give several concerts.

'I was suddenly enveloped by a sense of alarm,' he said. 'Something began to ache and trouble me. With every minute, the feeling of alarm increased. I was overcome by a powerful impulse to leave the city immediately. It became so strong in me that for the first and only time in my career, I cancelled all my local performances and left for Moscow without delay. Three days later, Ashkhabad was levelled by a devastating earthquake. Fifty thousand people were killed.'

But despite his extraordinary predictive ability, Messing was taken by surprise by his own death, which occurred when, living alone and in apparently good health, he was laid low by a fatal stroke. He was seventy-five years old.

Chapter 3
Clairvoyance

Clairvoyance ('clear-seeing') or, as it was named by F. W. H. Myers, one of the founders of the Society for Psychical Research, *telaesthesia*, is the direct knowledge of external events by the mind. Typically, the events are either viewed inwardly or are seen as visible apparitions. Yet sometimes, however, the information is perceived audibly, as when a voice recounts the details of a happening, when it is called *clairaudience*. More recently, the term *clairsentience* has been used to describe the act of being guided, often away from danger, by a strong feeling, or on occasion by invisible hands. These modern terms were all previously covered by the ubiquitous *second sight*, or 'knowledge of the unknowable'.

Clairvoyance has a very long tradition and has been reported from all parts of the world. Indeed, it is perhaps the most commonly experienced psychic manifestation. And while there have always been those who are especially sensitive in this respect, the evidence suggests that anyone can have a clairvoyant experience if the moment is right for it to happen. But it is worth remarking that our clairvoyant faculties are diminished by our modern lifestyle, for it is commoner among those who lead simpler and more rustic lives.

However, primitive tribal groups usually had a professional seer or clairvoyant, known as a shaman or witch-doctor, who was able, by dancing and beating a drum, to stimulate his psychic powers and precipitate a vision, which enabled him to locate a lost object, or discover the whereabouts of game or an absent tribesman. In fact not only were most shamans chosen before they reached puberty, but they were recognized by their hysterical or nervous temperament, and by their ability to pass certain tests, such as walking on hot coals without being burned and, conversely, being able to withstand immersion in freezing water.

But the tribal clairvoyant did not necessarily need to beat his drum or dance to gain information psychically, as this often came to him spontaneously. Olive Chapman tells of how the Swedish historian Johan Scheffer, writing in 1637 about the Lapps, severely reprimanded one who he had learned possessed a drum. 'The man brought the drum to Scheffer, confessing with tears in his eyes that even if he parted with it, it would make no difference for he would continue to have visions, for "he knew not how to make use of his eyes, since things altogether distant were presented to them". To prove his point he then accurately described to Scheffer all that had happened to him during his journey in Lapland.'

That clairvoyant perception is inhibited by modern life was realized as long ago as the eighteenth century. It is therefore to the credit of Samuel Johnson and James Boswell that they tried, on visiting the Hebrides where clairvoyance was apparently an endemic skill, to learn as much about it as they could.

'We should have had little claim to the praise of curiosity,' commented Johnson in his *A Journey to the Western Isles of Scotland*, 'if we had not endeavoured with particular attention to examine the question of the *Second Sight*.'

He went on to explain: 'The *Second Sight* is an impression made either by the mind upon the eye, or by the eye upon the mind, by which things distant or future are perceived and seen as if they were present. A man on a journey far from home falls from his horse; another, who is perhaps at work about the house, sees him bleeding on the ground, commonly with a landscape of the place where the accident occurs.' Yet while remarkable, the good doctor knew that clairvoyance 'is neither voluntary or constant. The appearances have no dependence upon choice: they cannot be summoned, detained, or recalled. The impression is sudden, and the effect often painful.'

But despite the pair's eagerness to find out more, they quickly discovered that they had neither the time to track down the source of the stories, nor the expertise to interview those concerned. 'To talk with any of these seers is not easy,' Johnson lamented. 'There is one living in Sky(*sic*), with whom we would gladly have conversed; but he was very gross and ignorant, and knew no English.' Hence they left the islands somewhat disappointed, Johnson admitting that 'I never could advance my curiosity to conviction; but came away at last only willing to believe.'

The implied difference between the shaman and the ordinary person is that while the latter experiences clairvoyant visions but rarely, the former is able to exploit his intuitive abilities as and when required. Yet this does not mean that the ordinary person lacks these abilities, only that they have not been encouraged to develop. People are often frightened by such abilities, and this inhibits them. 'It is an involuntary affection,' noted Johnson. 'Those who profess to feel it do not boast of it as a privilege, nor are they considered by others as advantageously distinguished. They have no temptation to feign; and their hearers have no motive to encourage imposture.'

You may like to investigate your own clairvoyant capacities using a deck of Zener cards. In the first experiment you will need the assistance of a partner, while in the second you will not.

Clairvoyance Test One

Let us assume that you are to be the subject, your partner the assistant. Have him sit at a table with the Zener card deck. You may sit opposite him, and you will need a pencil and a pad upon which you can record your results. When you feel ready to start, have the assistant shuffle the Zener cards well and then lay them face down in a pile on the table in front of him. He must then remove the top card and, without looking at it, lay it on the table to start a new pile. You will then try to identify, by clairvoyance, the symbol the card bears. Record what you think it is, and let your assistant know that you are ready to attempt the next card. He should place it on the first card, and you will again try to identify its symbol clairvoyantly. Again record your guess. Then continue in this manner down through the whole deck.

Check your score by having your assistant call out the order of the symbols, and tick those that you guessed correctly. Again, chance alone will give you five correct guesses. The more you get right, the greater will be the odds against chance being responsible, and this is suggestive of clairvoyance. Do at least five run-throughs and work out your average score.

Clairvoyance Test Two

This test is essentially the same as the first, the difference being that it allows you to work alone if an assistant is not available. Sit at a table equipped with a deck of Zener cards, a pad and pencil. Shuffle the cards well, and set them on the table before you. Then, when you feel relaxed and receptive, work your way down through the pack, clairvoyantly trying to sense the symbol on each card in it. Do not touch the cards while you do this. Record each symbol that you pick up. Next, check your score. Then do a few more run-throughs and average your score.

When Dr J. B. Rhine began his card-guessing experiments in the 1930s, his subjects were volunteer Duke University students and members of his own staff. His early clairvoyance trials, however, were largely negative, which both surprised and disappointed him. But this situation changed when a student named Hubert Pearce, whose mother was psychically sensitive, began to record high scores. Indeed, Pearce scored an average of ten correct guesses per run-through – five more than chance – and even, on one occasion, recorded twenty-five hits out of twenty-five, a result that gave odds of millions to one against chance.

Remarkable though Hubert Pearce was at card-guessing, his youthful talent proved a fickle friend, for on getting some worrying news from home, his clairvoyant skills evaporated, never to return. His scores, however, give you a measure of excellence against which you can judge yourself. If you score five correct guesses on average, your clairvoyant ability is non-existent or repressed. An average of six or seven correct guesses indicates a modest clairvoyant ability. Higher scores are indicative of a marked talent, while an average correct score of ten puts you up there with the champions!

When I discussed card-guessing scores in the first chapter, I said that scores higher than chance represented a positive deviation and scores lower than chance a negative deviation.

If you think about it, a score lower than that suggested by chance is as interesting in its own way as a score higher than chance. Such a score should not in fact occur; that it does is paradoxically also indicative of clairvoyance or ESP.

In fact, when the ESP researcher Gertrude Schmeidler discovered that two of her subjects, both of whom were quite sure that extra-sensory perception was nonsense, consistently scored below chance, while the rest, who were more open in their opinions, scored above the chance level, she called the former 'goats' and the latter 'sheep'. Over the next ten years she investigated this attitude factor very carefully in over one thousand subjects, and was to conclude that the sheep on average scored slightly above chance, and the goats on average slightly below.

Now why should this be? Well, consider the object of the experiment from the goats' point of view. They disbelieve in ESP, often to the extent of being downright hostile to it. Thus they do not want to achieve a positive score, as this would be slapping themselves in the face. 'Therefore,' noted Dr Schmeidler, 'it looks as if, consciously or unconsciously, they were using ESP to avoid the correct response.' And this is why a negative deviation from chance is as suggestive of ESP as a positive deviation.

You will of course know your own feelings about extra-sensory perception, which will tell you if you are a sheep or a goat. If you have bought this book and are using it, you will almost certainly be a sheep, and this indicates that you will score above chance in the clairvoyance tests described above. But if you have other people do the tests, make a special note of the scores of those who consider clairvoyance 'nonsense'. They may well score below chance.

Another personality type to be looked out for when testing for extra-sensory perception, is the 'psi-inhibitor'. This is a person who, although not necessarily hostile to the idea of ESP, in some way prevents it from manifesting in others. Psi-inhibitors do not cause a negative deviation from chance, but they will stop anyone from scoring above the chance level. If you find that your own scores stay frustratingly at the chance level, it may be because your partner or someone in your home is a psi-inhibitor. The remedy is obvious.

A person's psychological type is also relevant to the score that he or she obtains. It has been shown that, on average, extroverts get higher scores in ESP tests than introverts. Thus if you label yourself as being an outgoing, friendly type, you should perform better than if you are inward-looking and reserved. But perhaps the most important factor is your mood at the time when you do the tests. If you feel happy and relaxed, you will score better than if your mood is the opposite. A positive score will also be helped by the absence of distracting sounds (for example, passing traffic or overflying aircraft), a warm temperature and a comfortable chair. In a similar way, use of the Ganzfeld technique, which was described in Chapter One, also stimulates clairvoyant receptiveness.

Boredom and tiredness likewise inhibit our psychic abilities, and this is probably why most ESP researchers have noted a 'decline effect' when conducting card-guessing and similarly repetitive experiments. With some individuals the slump in positive scoring happens quickly, whereas with others the scores remain high for a lot longer and then decline.

It will perhaps interest you to monitor your own feelings to card-guessing as you do it yourself. The first two or three run-throughs will probably prove interesting, as they are a new experience which teaches you something new about yourself. But by the time you get to the fourth, fifth or sixth trial, the novelty will have worn off and the procedure will have become somewhat tedious. You may even wish that you had not started it. And that's when your scores will start to slump, when you will experience the decline effect.

Again, the remedy is obvious. As soon as the procedure starts to pall, take a break and relax. Only resume the experiment when you genuinely feel that you would like to have another go. Otherwise your efforts will be counter-productive.

The mentalist Wolf Messing was afraid of thunderstorms and could not function psychically when one was taking place, just as his successor Tofik Dadashev is inhibited when he is near high-powered radio and television aerials. Such disruption by electro-magnetic signals contrasts with the ancient belief that prophetic inspiration is stimulated by living near, or better still sleeping under, waterfalls.

This immediately suggests that positive ions, which are created by thunderstorms and in the vicinity of electrical generators, radio and television stations, industrial works, etc., lower psychic functioning, while negative ions, which are notably generated by running water, boost it. Indeed, research has shown this to be true. Thus negative ions are psi-maximizers.

This discovery offers you a proven way of stimulating your own ESP abilities, by working in a high negative ion environment. Because negative ions tend to accumulate in well-ventilated, unoccupied rooms, for instance, you will find it helpful to do your ESP tests in such a room, rather than in one that has been recently occupied. Negative ions are also present in greater numbers in the air of bright, clear days, especially just after a rain shower, which accounts for the better spirits of people on such days, whereas the irritability and grumpiness of people on close, thundery days is caused by the higher level of positive ions. Thus you can expect better results in any ESP test on the first type of day, and worse results on the second type of day.

If you have the funds and would like to improve both your mood and your psi powers, then you should buy yourself a negative ion generator. This small electrical device will, for the cost of a few pennies a day, keep the atmosphere of your bedroom or workroom healthily alive with negative ions.

Our clairvoyant faculties also vary according to the time of day. For example, our ESP abilities tend to be sharpest in the evening or during the hours of darkness. Somewhat similarly, many clairvoyants claim that they are psychically more active when the moon is waxing, that is, growing in size from new to full, and less active when it is waning. Periods of sun spot activity also affect our psychic powers, possibly because they lead to an increase in the amount of positive ions in the atmosphere.

Certain chemical substances have been shown to induce psychic receptivity, the three commonest and most easily obtainable being caffeine, ethyl alcohol and nicotine; the first being present in tea and coffee, the second in alcoholic drinks, and the third in tobacco smoke. Indeed, coffee, alcoholic beverages and tobacco were all regarded as divine substances in the cultures where their use originated, as they were believed to ease communication between this world and the next. But they are most effective when they are taken occasionally, while their regular use fails to excite, because the body soon becomes habituated. Moreover, a high intake of alcohol inhibits psychic receptivity.

There is a long list of other substances that have been, and in some instances still are, employed by shamans, witch-doctors and the like, for their capacity of breaking down the barriers between this world and the next, or, in other words, stimulating extra-sensory perception, but because most of them are dangerous to use, poisonous or illegal, they are best left unmentioned.

But because the simplest psychic stimulant is an interest in the proceedings and in achieving positive results, you may find, if the decline effect has set in with the first two clairvoyance tests, that a more interesting test will reawaken your psychic powers.

Clairvoyance Test Three

This test can be conveniently done by obtaining several postcards, say ten, which illustrate a number of strongly contrasting landscapes – for example, a seaside, a river scene, moors, mountains, a forest, etc. – each of which is placed in an opaque envelope and sealed down. If you do this test on your own, next shuffle the envelopes thoroughly together and then select one of them at random. The latter is your target and you now have, by clairvoyance alone, to describe or identify the scene portrayed by the hidden card. Record your impressions. Then open the envelope and see if your guess was correct. Record the result. Next, place the postcard back in the envelope and repeat the procedure a further nine times. Because chance would only give you a correct score of one out of ten, a higher score than that is indicative of clairvoyance. But you would need to do several trials to draw any conclusions.

The test is more stimulating clairvoyantly because the scenes are in themselves more interesting than the five Zener card symbols. Because of this, you may find that your scores are better than those you obtained in the Zener card tests.

In fact this test is very similar to the large and successful clairvoyance experiment that was carried out by W. Whately Carington in the 1930s. For the experiment, Carington used ordinary people, who often lived in a distant town, as the percipients, while the target material consisted of drawings whose subject was selected by a random code.

Once the target picture had been drawn, it was pinned up in Carington's office at 7 p.m. and left overnight until 9.30 the following morning, when it was taken down and locked away. During that time the percipients had to make their own sketches of what their extra-sensory perception told them about it. Nine more drawings were hung up, one on each of the subsequent nine nights, to make a total of ten. Each percipient then mailed in his or her ten sketches, plus any supporting description that he or she felt was necessary.

Each of the percipient's ten sketches was given a code number, so that it could later be discovered at which picture it had been targeted. Then all the drawings from the percipients were shuffled together and given to an independent judge, along with the ten original drawings. He examined every sketch and decided whether it was sufficiently like the target drawing to be considered a 'hit' or whether it was a 'miss'. Because the judge did not know which sketches were aimed at which target drawings, he could only use their observable similarities as a guide.

The results, however, would only be useful if the judge's own idiosyncracies were allowed for, which meant compensating for the decisions of a strict judge, who only accorded a hit to sketches that closely resembled the target drawings, while allowing for those of a lenient judge, who gave a hit label to sketches that perhaps only bore a slight resemblance to the original. This Carington accomplished in an original and thoughtful way.

Let us suppose that a particular judge marks a hundred sketches as hits. The misses are then set aside and ignored. Of the hits, five are sketches of a cat, which is the subject of one of the target drawings. We do not know, of course, on which night or nights those cats were sketched, but we would be acting permissively if we considered each of the cat sketches to have been prompted by chance. This means that on the night when the cat drawing was the target, we would have expected chance to have accounted for five per cent of the hits. But if, however, there are significantly more or less hits than five per cent on that night, then some other cause than chance must be responsible, which implies that clairvoyance (or possibly telepathy) was responsible for the result.

Indeed, in Whately Carington's seven principal experiments, involving a total of 741 people, he concluded that a weak extra-perceptive sense is possessed by the population at large.

But another interesting finding did emerge from Carington's results. He noticed that very often a hit was recorded not on the night that the target drawing was displayed, but on either the previous night or the succeeding night. That is, the percipients were sometimes scoring above chance on both the drawing of the previous night and on the drawing of the night to come, the former being indicative of retrocognition and the latter of precognition or foresight.

This 'displacement effect' has been also noticed by other psychical researchers like Dr J. B. Rhine, and indeed it is something that you should be aware of in your own experimental results.

It was during the 1930s that the mathematician Dr S. G. Soal, hoping to repeat the results of Dr Rhine, carried out a very large card-guessing experiment over a five-year period, which involved 160 subjects, who made a total of 128,350 guesses, but with the unfortunate result that only a chance result was obtained. When Carington heard of Soal's disappointing result, he suggested to Soal that he should re-examine his figures for any sign of the displacement effect. This Soal did, and found, or so he claimed, that two of his subjects, Basil Shackleton and Gloria Stewart, had scored above chance both backwards and forwards in time.

But, regretfully, Soal's displacement effect results were not allowed to stand, because not only did one independent observer catch him altering his figures, but a computer expert, Betty Hardwick, later found definite evidence of data manipulation. Hence Soal's results have been discredited.

In his book *ESP Research Today*, the psychic researcher J. Gaither Pratt, who worked at Duke University with Dr Rhine, quotes several quite dramatic examples of extra-sensory perception in action. Here, for instance, is the experience of an American woman:

'I lived fourteen miles from Memphis, Tennessee,' she said. 'One day I went to town to see a movie. I had an uneasy feeling as I entered the movie that something was on fire at home. This feeling grew until I could endure it no longer. I left the movie with an overpowering pull that drove me homeward.

'Within a mile of home I saw the fields all black and smoking. A boy hunting rabbits had thrown a lighted match in a field and started a fire. It took the fire department and fifty volunteers to save my home.'

A somewhat similar, although much more famous, incident involving fire, was recorded by the philosopher Immanuel Kant. The percipient was the mystic and theologian Emmanuel Swedenborg, who in July 1759 visited a country house in Göteborg, some three hundred miles from Stockholm, where he had his home. Kant says:

'About 6 p.m. Swedenborg left the company for a short while and returned looking pale and alarmed. He said that a dangerous fire had broken out in Sodermain in Stockholm, where his own house stood. He was restless, and went out several times. He said that the house of a certain friend, whom he named, was already in ashes, and that his own house was in danger. At 8 p.m. he again came in after a short absence and said that the fire had been quenched at the third door from his house . . . On the next day a messenger arrived who had left Göteborg while the fire was going on. He brought letters with him in which the conflagration was described in a way that tallied with Swedenborg's statements. On Tuesday morning the royal courtier from Stockholm arrived at the Governor's house with a precise statement that the fire had been put out at 8 p.m. that Saturday.'

The third and last example also in part concerns a fire. It was recorded by the Greek historian Herodotus, and takes us back much further in time, to the reign of the Lydian king Croesus. In about 548 BC Croesus, worried about the increasing power of the Persians under Cyrus, decided to consult one of the oracles for advice. But he first resolved to test several of the more famous, in order to ascertain which was the most accurate.

'The Lydians whom Croesus sent to make the tests were given the following orders,' writes Herodotus in *The Histories:* 'On the hundredth day, reckoning from the day on which they left Sardis, they were to consult the oracles, and inquire what Croesus, son of Alyattes and king of Lydia, was doing at that moment. The answer of each oracle was to be taken down in writing and brought back to Sardis.'

What Croesus actually did on the hundredth day was to cut up a tortoise and a lamb and boil them together in a bronze cauldron with a bronze lid. He was therefore understandably impressed with what the Delphic priestess, the Pythia, told his men.

> 'I count the grains of sand on the beach and measure the sea;
> I understand the speech of the dumb and hear the voiceless.
> The smell has come to my sense of a hard-shelled tortoise
> Boiling and bubbling with lamb's flesh in a bronze pot:
> The cauldron underneath is of bronze, and of bronze the lid.'

Each of these three remarkable happenings, while certainly demonstrative of extra-sensory perception, can perhaps more specifically be called clairvoyant. However, we cannot completely rule out telepathy, because other human beings were involved in all the incidents. But even though there is this complication, which adds weight to Rhine's feeling that 'it now seems doubtful whether they (i.e. telepathy and clairvoyance) are two different processes at all', these three examples show that extra-sensory perception operates equally successfully at distances as varied as fifteen miles, two hundred and eighty miles (that between Sardis and Delphi) and three hundred miles.

The phenomenon of clairaudience is as interesting as, but perhaps more important than, clairvoyance. Simply expressed, it is the paranormal hearing of sounds like voices, music, thunder, gun-fire, etc., which have no physical source, and which are often not heard by those with the percipient. Yet while clairaudience has been reported throughout history, it is rarely admitted to nowadays, because it has come, as Brian Inglis points out in *The Paranormal*, 'to be regarded as an indication of incipient insanity'.

It is true, nonetheless, that schizophrenics and other mentally deranged people frequently claim that God, the Devil, spirits or deceased persons like Napoleon speak to them, although this does not mean that all those who hear voices, whether occasionally or often, are mentally ill.

To understand this, we must consider how our brains function auditorily. The sound that we ordinarily hear when someone speaks or a dog barks is not 'out there' in the sense that it is just piped into our brains via our ears. Such sounds do not have an objective reality; rather, we create them in the hearing centres of our brains from the auditory impulses that are produced in the inner ear by vibrations in the air, the sound waves. To make this clear, ask yourself if a dog whistle makes a sound when it is blown. To you it doesn't, but to the dog – which is sensitive to sound waves of a higher frequency – it does. In other words, a sound has no reality outside the brain that hears it, which effectively gives an answer to that age-old question: does a palm tree, falling over in the desert miles from any living thing, make a sound when it hits the ground?

Hence when we hear a sound that has no outside source, it can only mean that the hearing centres of the brain have been activated, either by a mental malfunction or by a paranormal stimulus. The latter results in clairaudience.

One interesting example of clairaudience was reported by Louisa Rhine. It happened to a young man who had started work at a Wisconsin department store, which had taken him four hundred miles away from his home and his mother. One day while he was serving a customer he suddenly heard his mother call out to him, and without thinking he turned and replied: 'Yes, mother?' He was both surprised and embarrassed to discover that his mother was not there, and could only apologetically explain to the customer that he had seemingly heard his mother speak to him.

Nonplussed, he wrote to his mother and described what had happened. 'She wrote back,' the young man said, 'that on that very day she was in the garden and wanted a hoe, and had apparently forgotten I wasn't at home and turned towards the house and called me, fully expecting an answer. Then she realized I was gone and felt funny about it – but wasn't it strange that I heard and answered her four hundred miles away?'

This incident may have been caused by the mother's thoughts telepathically stimulating her son's hearing centres, thereby producing the illusion that she had called him from nearby.

Clairaudiently heard voices may belong to those who are living, as in the case mentioned above, or who are dead – or they may apparently originate from a spiritual entity. The voice may, at its simplest, merely call out the person's name, or it may offer advice, warn of danger or even predict the future.

The Greek philosopher Socrates was frequently counselled by a voice he called his *daimon* or deity, which helped him to make the right decisions and live correctly. When he was condemned to death for supposedly corrupting the youth of Athens, he told the jury: 'In the past the prophetic voice to which I have become accustomed has always been my constant companion . . . yet neither when I left home this morning, nor when I was taking my place here in the court, nor at any point in any part of my speech did the divine sign oppose me. In other discussions it has often checked me in the middle of a sentence; but this time it has never opposed me in any part of this business in anything I have said or done. What do I suppose to be the explanation? I will tell you. I suspect that this thing that has happened to me is a blessing, and we are quite mistaken in supposing death to be an evil. I have good grounds for thinking this, because my accustomed sign could not have failed to oppose me if what I was doing had not been sure to bring some good result.'

Joan of Arc, the maid of Orleans, was another historical personage who received guidance from discarnate voices. These began talking to her when she was sixteen years of age, and were to encourage her to take up arms against the English invaders of France. That she, an illiterate peasant girl, should thereafter not only gain command of the French Army, but drive the English from Orleans and herself crown the Dauphin king, all acts that the voices had prophesied she would accomplish, suggests that they were not caused by mental derangement, but came, as they themselves said, from the spirit world.

Indeed, the teenage years appear to be the most important where ESP is concerned. If those who possess psychic powers are helped to develop them, as happens in primitive societies, then they can be turned into remarkable people, like shamans, medicine men and witch-doctors. But because modern society has no need of such people, whose abilities are derided as superstitious nonsense, encouragement is lacking and the latent abilities fail to bloom. Or, if the ability is sufficiently strong but the teenager is forced to deny it, it may manifest as poltergeist activity, which is invariably associated with a 'disturbed' adolescent.

In Native American culture, which implicitly believed in a spirit world, every young boy and girl was expected to acquire a spirit guide, who would remain with them throughout life and give them a certain power, the most talented in this respect becoming medicine men and women. The guardian spirit quest usually took place between the ages of ten and fourteen, when the child was told: 'It is time for you to fast and seek your spirit guide. It will give you your special power and be your guide throughout all your life. You will call upon it whenever you need it. *Unless you find it when you are a boy, you cannot become much of a man.'*

Although the details of the quest differed from tribe to tribe, what usually happened was this: the boy or girl was first made to bathe, and was afterwards sent to a special place, such as a bear's den if he or she wished for bear power or to the top of a mountain if eagle power was sought, where he or she would remain all alone without eating for several days or weeks, until the spirit revealed itself, which it often did when the child was asleep. The spirit gave the child a special name, a song and a power. These were kept secret until the time was right for them to be revealed, usually when he or she became an adult. Once this had happened, the individual would not only wear some sign of the spirit – for instance, a bear's claw or an eagle's feather – but could then call upon the power he or she had been given, when this was necessary, to heal the sick, to fight bravely, to hunt well, to speak wisely, etc. Yet not every child was granted a spirit vision at the first attempt, which meant that another or others had to be undertaken.

Some years ago farmer Lucullus McWhorter recorded the following account told him by Yellow Wolf, a Nez Pearce Indian, of his second guardian spirit quest, the first having proved unsuccessful.

'When I was a boy of about thirteen snows, my parents sent me off into the hills, to find my *Wyakin*, my guardian spirit . . . this time I was sent to the wildest part of the mountains. I carried only one blanket but no food. I could drink all the water I wanted. My only shelter was trees, and I slept on fir branches. I was told to stay in one place three or four or five moons and then go somewhere else. I might have to be gone fifteen or twenty moons, all alone, without food. I had no weapon, for nothing would harm me. No child ever got hurt when looking for his guardian spirit.

'After many suns without food, I slept and had something like a dream. You white people call it a trance. A figure stood in front of me and talked to me. "My boy, look at me. Take a good look at me! If you do what I tell you to do, you will be as I am. I will give you my power. You may think I am nothing. You may think that I am only bones, but I am alive. You can see me now. I am Hemene Moxmox."

'It was the spirit of a wolf that was talking to me. Its colour was a sort of yellow, and it seemed to float in the air. It talked to me like a human being, and it gave me its power . . .

'That is how I got the name Yellow Wolf. I was named for the vision-wolf that appeared to me. It gave me the power to be a warrior. Following its directions, I made a war-club when I was still a boy. This war-club gave me the killing strength of thunder. So I am sometimes called "White Thunder" and sometimes "White Lightning".'

Clairaudient experiences often happen in times of danger, when the discarnate voice will suggest a line of action to be taken or a direction to move in, which will preserve the person concerned.

One of the best known of such experiences happened to the escapologist Harry Houdini, when, having extricated himself from handcuffs and a container under the ice of the frozen Hudson River, he was unable to locate the exit hole in the ice – until his mother's voice, calling out his name, showed him the right direction to take.

In the chapter titled 'Supernatural Rescues' in his book *Life After Life*, Dr Raymond Moody recounts the story told him by a man who had been accidentally trapped in a large vat into which hot acid and steam were being pumped under high pressure.

'I could not see,' the man said, 'and the heat was so intense that I could not open my eyes. I had my eyes closed the whole time. But it seemed that the whole area was lit up with a glow. And a verse of Scripture that I had heard all my life, that had never meant much to me, "Lo, I am with thee always", came from the direction which later turned out to be the only way out . . . the fact that it came from the direction it came from and that I followed the voice was why I came out alive.'

A Korean friend of mine, Yung Bum Whang, told me of a similar experience that had happened to an uncle of his, whose ship had come under Communist shell-fire in East Korea Bay. He was knocked down and stunned when the ship was hit, but then heard a mysterious voice say to him, "Quick, move to the other side of the ship." He struggled to his feet and did as the voice commanded. Moments later, a shell struck the deck where he had been lying and would certainly have killed him had he not moved.

Another friend, Donald S., was likewise saved by a voice when the merchant vessel Frederika Lensen, on which he was the radio officer, was torpedoed by a German U-boat on 20 July 1942, as it sailed down the St Lawrence River bound for Britain. Just before the torpedo exploded in the engine room and split the ship in two, a voice warned him to move away from the doorway where he was standing and under which the rupture in the ship's plating appeared. He believes that the voice saved him from serious injury or death.

But helpful though such voices are to those who hear them, it must be wondered why those who don't are not so lucky. After all, four men died in the engine room of the Frederika Lensen, who would perhaps still be alive today if a voice had told them to get up on deck. The answer must be that either those who were killed had reached the moment when they were fated to die, or that their ESP was insufficiently developed to allow such guidance.

Which brings us to the less well-known, but equally fascinating, extra-sensory experience known as clairsentience. This often involves the touching and holding of a person by 'ghostly' hands which direct that person, perhaps to the extent of saving his or her life.

Here, for example, is what happened to Mrs E. E. West in December 1937, after she had lost a ruby from her gold ring while doing some washing. Thinking that the ruby had gone down the plug hole, she gave it up for lost. But on the following day, while she was in the same room, a voice said to her: 'What about the ruby?'

'Oh, that's gone for good, it's no use troubling about that,' she replied without thinking.

'By that time I realized that I was replying to no visible person but, before I could think further, I seemed to be grasped by the shoulders and twisted around, and the first thing my eyes rested upon was the ruby on the floor shining in a shaft of sunlight made by the outside door being open a crack. I do not wish it to be thought that I felt my shoulders grasped, any more than I heard a particular person's voice, but that I was aware of myself as a person inside my body, but the same shape, which heard and felt quite well without my body.'

And Yellow Wolf, the Nez Pearce Indian mentioned above, was once roused by the touch of his *Wyakin*, after he had fallen asleep while guarding some horses on a freezing night.

'Riding horseback, I was doubled over and my eyes were closed because of the cold wind. I went sound asleep. I did not know anything and I must have been near death, when I felt something lightly touch my thigh and shake it. Then I heard a voice speaking – "What are you doing? Wake up! You are dead! Go home!"'

Sometimes other physical impressions are sensed. I myself have often felt, when meditating, what seemed to be a cool breeze drift lightly across my face, and once I heard the fluttering of wings as though a bird had flown two or three times around my head. A later search of the room revealed no bird or any place where a bird might have entered or left it. And a few weeks after my Great Pyrenees dog had died, I woke up in the night and felt her apparently lying with her back against mine, as she often did when she thought she could get away with it.

Lastly, we may say that clairvoyant, clairaudient and clairsentient impressions are most often experienced when we are in an altered state of consciousness, as when we are asleep, in a trance, meditating or are hypnotized. And this applies as much to those who have a psychic talent, as to those who do not. Spontaneous psychic impressions, as when Swedenborg became aware of the fire in Stockholm, are generally forced on the consciousness by dramatic events, like a death or a disaster, and then only occasionally.

We shall be considering sleep, dreams and hypnosis in later chapters. But we must first consider the practical use of clairvoyance in dowsing.

Chapter 4
Dowsing

Although nobody quite knows how dowsing works, dowsers or 'water-witches' are active in many countries, such as the United States, Canada and the Soviet Union, where they are employed to find underground water, oil, piping and cables, mineral deposits, missing persons, etc. Hence dowsing is essentially the art of finding hidden things, especially things hidden or buried in the ground.

The typical dowser works with a divining rod. The traditional rod is a forked or Y-shaped stick cut from a tree like hazel, willow or apple. The dowser grasps the two arms of the Y, so that the stem of the rod points forwards and slightly upwards. The arms are held under a certain amount of tension, the hands gripping the rod so that it is able to pivot.

The dowser then walks across the area of land where he believes the water, oil or whatever might be, while at the same time keeping a clear image of what he is seeking in his mind. When he is over the spot where the substance he is looking for lies, the rod moves either upwards or downwards, thus indicating by its movement, the position of the hidden substance.

Dowsing can be much more specific than simply indicating that the desired substance is there. Drilling or mining operations are very costly, and the skilled dowser has to be able to provide more information than the mere fact of the substance's existence. For instance, a farmer who wants to pump water for his cattle from an underground stream does not want to dig a deep well down to a thin dribble of polluted water.

'A good dowser can determine the direction of the water flow, its depth, and give a reliable estimate of its volume and pressure,' says Bruce Sullivan, a member of the board of trustees of the American Dowsers Association and a founder-member of Thought Technology Limited. 'And a very skilled dowser can tell if the water is drinkable or not. He is also able to give similar information about buried oil or mineral deposits.'

It has been suggested that a dowser is sensitive to minute magnetic variations in the ground beneath his feet, which are produced by the buried substance. If so, the magnetic variations could cause his arm muscles to twitch and in turn prompt the movement of the rod. This idea has received some support from experiments carried out in Russia, which have shown that a dowser's ability to locate buried objects is lost if he has magnets attached to his wrists or back.

By this token the divining rod is merely an indicator, not the means by which the hidden substance is found. The human body is the receiver. Indeed, some people are able to dowse with their hands alone, which twitch like a rod when the right spot is found.

'But there is no really satisfactory explanation for dowsing,' comments Sullivan. 'In fact it's probable that several different energies are involved.'

That it is not the rod which is doing the work is also suggested by the wide use of different materials and rod shapes for divining. For example, dowsers have used scissors, pieces of bone, walking sticks and even clay pipes as divining rods, although the most popular alternative to the traditional hazel or willow rod are metal L-rods, which can be cut and made from wire coat-hangers.

If you make a pair of metal L-rods (see Figure 5), there is nothing to stop you testing your own dowsing abilities in the garden. With your arms bent at the elbow, hold the rods pointing forwards and lying parallel to each other. Grip them lightly so that they can easily swivel in your hands. If you now walk slowly across your garden lawn, thinking of 'the water pipe' or 'the electricity cable' or whatever, you may find that when you get to the place where it is, the rods will either swing together or swing outwards. You should first try locating a hidden cable or pipe whose course you know, or something whose position you can later check on the house plan. Otherwise you'll have to dig a hole or holes in the lawn, which will detract from the charm of the exercise.

But while the notion that the human body responds to magnetic variations in the ground is a neat, scientific concept, it cannot be the whole explanation. For there is also the matter of map dowsing.

All professional diviners map dowse. This entails locating the position of the water or mineral deposit on a map before going out in the field. After all, a dowser might have to investigate several hundred acres of

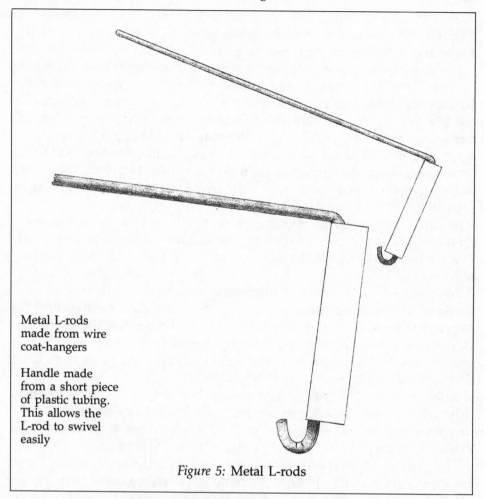

Metal L-rods
made from wire
coat-hangers

Handle made
from a short piece
of plastic tubing.
This allows the
L-rod to swivel
easily

Figure 5: Metal L-rods

ground to find what he is looking for, and to do this by walking or even driving around would be tedious and time-consuming.

Map dowsing allows the diviner to investigate the area quickly and cheaply. To do this he spreads out a map of the area in question and then goes over it with a pendulum, which is simply a small metal or glass weight hung at the end of a piece of fine string (see Figure 6, page 55).

'To do map work with a pendulum one should be seated comfortably and in a calm state of mind,' says Sullivan, 'and have the objective in clear mental focus. You also have to work within the limits imposed on you by

your client. For example, he'll want the well to be on or within a certain
distance of his property and, obviously, he won't be interested in boring
a well through five hundred feet of granite.'

The pendulum responds to the presence of the sought after substance
by either swinging from side-to-side or moving in a circular motion. A
side-to-side movement is perhaps best as the direction of swing indicates
the line on the map where the substance lies. Then, by moving the
pendulum to the opposite side of the map and waiting for it to swing
again, the site of the substance is marked by the point at which the two
lines cross. This technique, in cartography, is known as triangulation. The
dowser generally starts with small-scale maps and then switches to large-
scale maps as he homes in on his quarry.

It is only after he has located the position of the substance he is seeking
on the map that the dowser goes out into the field with his divining rod.
Then, if he verifies at the site that the substance is there, drilling or digging
will proceed.

But clearly, map dowsing cannot work in quite the same way as field
dowsing, if the latter functions by the dowser's muscles twitching in
response to underground magnetic variations. There are no such magnetic
variations on the paper surface of a map. Hence the dowser using a map
must be employing his psychic faculties. In other words, he appears to be
finding locations by means of clairvoyance.

Bruce Sullivan believes that everyone has innate dowsing abilities,
although he feels that women are particularly good at dowsing because
they are generally more sensitive to psychic impressions. He also thinks
that our dowsing talent is greatest when we are young.

'The general rule of thumb is that any child up to the age of about seven
can dowse quite easily,' he says. 'From about seven to twelve years of age
fifty per cent can. But after age twelve the number diminishes quite
quickly.'

But don't let this stop you from trying out your own dowsing talents with
either a divining rod or a pendulum. Who knows, your dowsing potential
might simply be waiting for a try-out!

And if you do try but can't seem to get anything happening, do what
many dowsers do to help tune themselves in psychically: hold a small
sample of the substance being sought while using the rod or the
pendulum.

However, be warned that if you discover that you are able to dowse, you probably won't be able to find items like gold or treasure. In fact dowsing for valuables, while theoretically possible, seldom works in practice. A dowser might of course be able to find oil or minerals that he can exploit for his own profit, but he has little chance of locating a treasure chest by dowsing.

The use of dowsing to find missing persons is a fascinating branch of the art. Missing persons should be located by map dowsing first, and then by going out in the field, as for water, oil and minerals. But locating dead

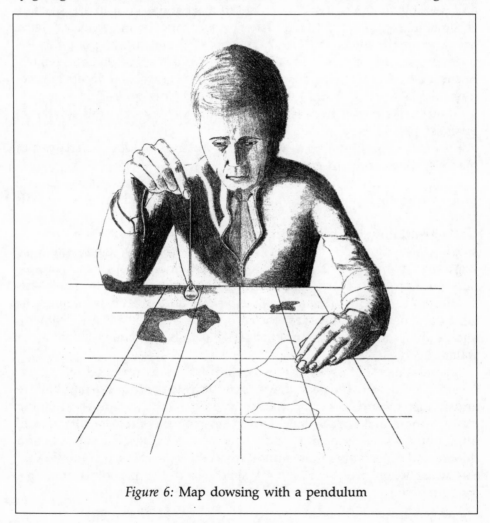

Figure 6: Map dowsing with a pendulum

bodies by field dowsing must depend upon clairvoyance, rather than upon the detection of magnetic variations, as corpses do not produce magnetic disturbances in their surroundings.

Sullivan claims that during the Vietnam War, the U.S. Army developed a rotary divining rod which was used with great success to locate not only Vietcong in the jungle but also the underground tunnels they had dug. Such work could be done from a moving jeep by specially-trained soldiers.

The Soviets have discovered that dowsing from the air is both practical and possible. It can be used as an aid to map dowsing or in areas where accurate maps are not available. The dowser works in an aeroplane flying over the area being investigated, and his divining rod responds in the normal way. In one test conducted by the Soviet researcher Nikolai Sochevanov, dowsers working in an aeroplane were able to locate a three-foot thick lead seam lying five hundred feet below ground level.

Sullivan has begun exploring another use of dowsing, the solving of business problems.

'I use dowsing as an executive decision-making tool for the analysis of markets, ideas and concepts,' he says.

Using a pendulum, Sullivan is able to check business decisions and probe the viability of other companies that seek to do business with his own.

'The pendulum can give me a "yes" answer on questions I put to it by starting to swing, and the intensity of the swing qualifies this,' he explains. 'Let's say I'm approached by a particular distributor who wants to handle one of our products and who is located some distance away. If I don't have the time or the information to evaluate his operation by the usual methods I can use a pendulum to assess the company's credibility, aggressiveness, and its ability to handle the product. It's basically the same as looking for water.'

He maintains that so far the pendulum has been very accurate.

Hence today, as in the past, dowsers continue to contribute to agriculture and industry by discovering water, oil and minerals – and by helping businessmen make decisions. How they achieve their results is still improperly understood, but with the discovery of new oil deposits and mineral lodes becoming more important as the years pass, it is certain that the 'water-witch' will be a highly visible part of the psychic scene for a long time yet.

Chapter 5
Psychometry

In the previous chapter it was mentioned that when a dowser goes over a map with a pendulum in order to pin-point the location of whatever he is searching for, he often finds it helpful to hold a small piece or a quantity of the substance being sought. This helps his clairvoyant faculties to 'tune-in' to the underground source or lode, which is then indicated by the movement of the pendulum.

Some psychics use objects in a similar way, not to find oil or minerals, but to discover information about the person or persons connected with it. They may, of course, sometimes be asked to locate a person who is missing, but they are more likely to be asked what the object reveals about the past, present and future of the person concerned.

This technique is commonly called 'psychometry' (literally 'the measurement of the mind'), an inaccurate term invented by the anthropologist Buchanan, although it is also referred to as 'psychoscopy' and, more straightforwardly, as 'object-reading'.

In principle, psychometry is easy to do, but in practice it is rather tricky, because its success depends entirely upon the sensitivity of the reader. Some people find images, ideas, names, odours, etc., float up easily into their conscious mind when they hold an object, while others get little or nothing at all. And while many psychometrists can only work with an object, like a ring or a pendant, that has been in contact with the subject's skin for some time, others get equally vivid impressions from an object that has only been briefly held or touched. Similarly, some psychometrists prefer the object to be made of metal, especially gold or silver, or from a precious stone; others, however, can 'read' objects made of wood, paper or fabric, etc., just as easily.

This naturally suggests that the psychometrist translates or deciphers some quality or energy from the object which was absorbed while it was worn or touched. But if so, it would leave unanswered the question of how the reader is so often able to look into the future, which presumably has not happened at the time the energy is absorbed.

And even more puzzling is the fact discovered by Dr Eugene Osty, the eminent French psychic investigator, that once the percipient has begun obtaining impressions from an object handed to him by a client, he can usually either give it back to him or otherwise dispense with it without interrupting the flow of information. Equally strange is the faculty possessed by some psychometrists of being able to receive impressions from a photograph that has been neither touched nor seen by the person portrayed in it. Indeed, the Dutch sensitive Peter Hurkos finds that he obtains his clearest impressions from a negative photograph, less clear ones from a positive print, and least information from a photocopy or a printed reproduction of the photograph.

Few psychometrists, however, visualize things exactly as they happen. The mind is not a cathode ray tube upon which scenes of the past, present and future are displayed with crystal clarity. More often it is the essence which is sensed, while the details are missed. In this respect it is pertinent to quote Dr Osty, who noted: 'In the course of my study of metagnomic (or psychic) subjects, I have never yet come across veridical hallucinations i.e. those which are identical to external reality. The visual images have always seemed to be reconstructions of ideas, of notions and of cognitions. If I have no warrant for denying the possibility of veridical hallucinations (understood as exact representations of reality), I am at least entitled by virtue of a long, active investigation to say that in practical research it is very rare, or at any rate only occurs with exceptional subjects.'

An example given by Dr Osty in his book *Supernormal Faculties of Man* (1923), and which happened to himself, illustrates this point perfectly. In March 1911, a sensitive told him: 'Take care, you will soon have a serious accident . . . I hear a violent shock . . . What luck! You will take no hurt! . . . I see a man bleeding on the ground; he is moaning and all around him some things are strewn; I can't say what.'

And this is what happened to Dr Osty on 15 August 1911:

'I was going at an easy pace in my car when a drunken baker, driving furiously, pulled the wrong rein and collided. The shock was such that the shaft, which struck the frame in the front glass, was shivered in pieces and one wheel mounted the bonnet and crushed it in. My friend, Th.

Stennuit, and I were stricken with amazement at the suddenness of the accident and our good fortune at being unhurt. Turning round we saw the horse galloping off, the cart in the ditch, and the baker stretched moaning and bleeding in the middle of the road with a number of loaves scattered around him.'

To give you an idea of the range of information and the way in which it can appear to a psychometrist, here are the notes I took down while John Fleming of Hastings, Sussex, read the ankh pendant that I gave him to hold in August 1974:

'Difficult five or six years; very independent, loving person; three years ago cut away from people; like England; back in four years; may change publisher in the middle of next year; links with Scotland; like country, open air; may go to Scotland . . . South Africa . . . Greece; force guiding writing; becomes more inspirational; trouble with right knee in October/November; don't put eggs all in one basket; start business venture in one year; like old country churches; will visit centre of England/North Wales to do an article or book on witchcraft; return to England in eight or nine months, three-quarters work, one-quarter pleasure; must be master of own ship; stay out of business until latter part of 1975; way with animals; have healing powers (see you in white coat healing animals/people); trouble at bottom of right lung; lady who sells flowers, roses; increase for next seven years; will speak to lady from the spirit world on October or November 10th; check steering on van, will change it in three or four months; eat venison; Switzerland; may need glasses for right eye towards Easter; quite a lot of money in Easter 1976; wife, a strong person, impulsive; stepfather, a man of few words, has spine trouble.'

This is very much a mixture of character description, likes, potential health problems, advice, past and future activities and happenings, and so on. In 1974, when the reading was done, I was living in Montreal, Canada, which had been my home since 1969, and those five years, as Fleming said, had been difficult. The biggest upset had occurred in the summer of 1974, when I had taken my landlord to court in an action that became something of a *cause célèbre* with the Montreal conservation lobby, whose interests I was representing (see *Montreal at the Crossroads*, by Donna Gabeline, Dane Lanken and Gorden Pape; Harvest House Publishers, 1975). And the name of the rogue landlord? It was, coincidentally, John Fleming! And yes, I did return unexpectedly to England in 1978; there was a change of publisher in the sense that a book of mine initially published by Zebra Books of New York was also brought out by Pinnacle Books; and the fact that my wife was born in Scotland gave me a link with that country. My supposed likes are all correct. I did visit Scotland in 1975 and 1976, and Greece in 1979 and 1980, but I have not yet been to South Africa. I did return to England for a visit nine months later, which was mainly devoted to researching articles and which took me to Leicester in the centre of England, but not to North Wales. I did write an article about witchcraft at the end of 1974, but it was based on a coven practising in Montreal. I did not change my van; rather, I was obliged to get rid of it in December 1974, when an unexpected cold snap cracked its block. I don't know if I have healing powers, but I once spent a lot of time in a white coat as I had previously been a biology teacher. I did attend several spiritualist churches early in 1975, but not as early as October/November 1974. There was a general increase, I suppose, during the following seven years, but the cutting away from people three years previously, the business venture, the trouble with my right eye, right lung and right knee, eating venison, going to Switzerland and gaining quite a lot of money at Easter 1976 were all wrong. And while my wife was a strong person, my stepfather was not a man of few words, quite the opposite in fact, and neither did he have spine trouble.

I will give John Fleming a 65 per cent correct score for that reading, which was not at all bad considering that he knew nothing about me and had derived all his information either directly from the ankh or through whatever subconscious channel it had opened up for him. He also had to work under the disadvantage of a strange setting – the reading was done at my aunt's house – and on a summer afternoon, neither of which favoured his psychic sensitivity.

You may now feel ready to test your own powers of 'object-reading'. If so, you will find that you achieve the best results in a familiar environment where you won't be disturbed. You should also be in a relaxed mood and have nothing worrying you. And while you can read any object, you should ideally work with something given to you by a friend who knows its history. And if you psychometrize with your friend, he can both take notes and give you an encouraging 'yes' when you make a statement he knows to be true.

When you are seated comfortably take the object in your fingers and just feel it. Feel its shape, its texture, its temperature and its other physical features. Then shut your eyes, relax and clear your mind. Now let any images, ideas, feelings and other associations which are generated by the object float up into your consciousness. Such upwellings will not happen straight away, so be patient. In fact if you try and force the pace you may prevent anything happening at all. Yet once any images, etc., appear, accept them. Don't think to yourself 'That can't be true' or 'That's nonsense', and don't edit. You may find it helpful to become aware of several things before you say anything, or you may want to report on each separate idea or image. Then, when you think that you have received everything that the object can reasonably tell you – and this may not be much at first – take a few deep breaths, let your brain start to function normally again and open your eyes. Stay quiet for a few moments. Now let your friend tell you what he knows of the object and what he got from your reading. And while he does that you will be able to go through your own impressions of the object and see how they were starting to make sense.

Once you have taken a short break, try reading a new object. And after that read another one or two.

The idea of doing several readings is to give your extra-sensory faculties some exercise and to let you experience how different objects can precipitate different depths of response. Almost certainly you will discover that some objects are easier to read than others, and also that while one may prompt a largely visual reaction, another will create an idea or a feeling response.

Don't expect immediate success, although you will probably do better than you think. Psychometry requires the use of psychic faculties that may long have been dormant and which you cannot reasonably expect to leap into full activity. Rather, they will gradually come to life, and it will take them time to mature.

One of the most remarkable psychometrists of modern times is the Dutchman Peter Hurkos, whose psychic gifts have been used extensively by the police forces of several countries when their usual methods of detection have drawn a blank. In this respect Hurkos has become, like the late Gerard Croiset, a psychic detective. On many occasions he has been able, while holding an object associated with a crime, such as a piece of clothing or a weapon, to describe with uncanny accuracy the crime scene, the whereabouts of the victims if they are missing, and give a description of the criminal. He played an important role in the recovery of the Coronation Stone following its theft in 1950, in the Boston Strangler case of 1964 and in the Charles Manson killings of 1970.

Peter Hurkos' capabilities were investigated in the late 1950s by the parapsychologist Dr Andrija Puharich at his Maine laboratory. In one test carried out in 1958, Hurkos was sent a sealed package by Puharich's colleague Professor Durcasse of Brown University and asked to give his impressions of its contents. The package actually contained a small pottery jar that had been found at the Roman town of Pompeii, which was destroyed by a volcanic eruption in AD 79. The jar had been broken and repaired, and was purchased at Pompeii in 1922 by the late Dr Stevenson Smith. The following is a condensed account of what Hurkos said about the jar:

'This object blew up – an explosion. There was an explosion – a long time ago. I hear a strange language. It is very old. It had also to do with water. I don't know what it is. I see a dark colour. It is not straight, not regular. It is very jagged, sharp points. It belonged to three people. I am sure of this. Dr Durcasse didn't buy this. It was given to him, and it was repaired. A souvenir. I am sure that the owner of the cylinder is dead. I do not mean Dr Durcasse, he is well.'

Even though Hurkos was not able to specifically identify the hidden object as a jar, he could tell that it was cylindrical in shape, very old, foreign and had been involved in some cataclysmic event. He was also able to report on its recent history. However, he was not able to say anything more about it than was known by its present owner, Professor Durcasse. This suggested to Dr Puharich that the jar 'acted as a tuning device which allowed Hurkos to tap, in an approximate way, the mind of Dr Durcasse with specific reference to the object in hand'.

That psychometrists derive at least part of their information by telepathy or clairvoyance was convincingly demonstrated in the 1930s by Dr J. Hettinger. He ingeniously arranged that while a psychometrist handled an object, its owner, unbeknownst to the psychometrist, sat in a house several miles away reading an illustrated magazine like *Picture Post*. As Dr Hettinger took down what the psychometrist said about the object, the owner carefully recorded what he was looking at or reading in the magazine, and the time at which this was done. When Dr Hettinger later compared the psychometrist's statements with the pictures or text that the owner had been examining at the time, he found some obvious correspondences. For example, when the latter was looking at a photograph of a hospital patient whose head and arms were bandaged, the psychometrist said that she had received an impression of 'a coiled rope, heavily twisted around . . . Someone with an arm bandaged up; an accident.' And again, when the owner examined a picture of a girl in a gymnastic pose, the psychometrist revealed that she felt that the owner was 'in touch with someone who can twist the body anyhow'.

This indicates that the psychometrist is not extracting information from the object he is handling – that it has not, in some mysterious way, absorbed information energy from its owner – but is using his own telepathic, clairvoyant or precognitive powers to supply information about the owner. Hence the object is nothing more than a psychic stimulant or focus point, the 'tuning device' of Dr Andrija Puharich, which enables the psychometrist to utilize his own intuitive powers of insight and foresight, rather in the same manner that a scryer uses a crystal ball.

In other words, psychometry lets you use your ESP. If you find that you become good at it, then your powers of ESP are well-developed. The reverse, however, is not necessarily true, for if you do not seem to get anything from the objects you hold, this may be because they are not the correct vehicles for unlocking your psychic talents. Which means that you need to attempt another method that perhaps will.

Before we leave psychometry to consider precognition, we must examine 'dermo-optical perception' or eyeless-sight, the apparent ability to 'see' through certain areas of the skin, like the fingertips, palms, back of the neck, ear-lobes, etc. Those possessing this remarkable ability can not only identify colours and shapes, but can also read numbers, letters and even sentences through their skin.

Knowledge of dermo-optical perception is not particularly new. The nineteenth-century psychiatrist Cesare Lombroso (1836–1909) reported that one of his patients, a female hysteric, could 'see' with the tip of her nose and the lobe of her left ear. And in the 1920s the French writer Jules Romains, upon investigating the capacity of some sleepwalkers to negotiate obstacles and perform quite complex tasks, found that when awake they possessed a 'para-optical' ability which allowed them to both 'see' colours and read sentences through their fingertips and also other parts of their bodies.

Yet eyeless-sight remained a neglected human talent until the case of Rosa Kuleshova gained wide publicity in the 1960s. Since then it has been actively investigated, notably in the Soviet Union, where it is hoped that it may one day be used by the blind.

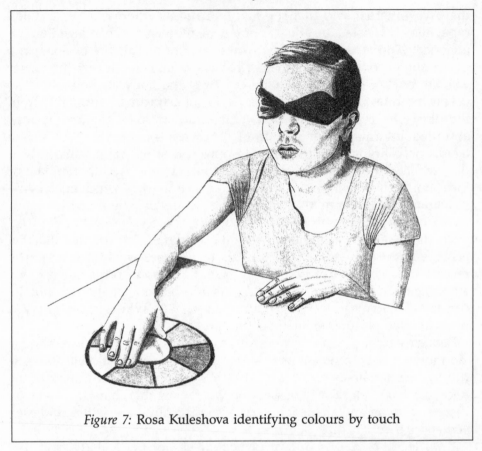

Figure 7: Rosa Kuleshova identifying colours by touch

Rosa Kuleshova, a schoolteacher in the Ural mountain town of Nizhni Tagil, first attracted attention when she demonstrated her extraordinary dermo-optical abilities to Dr I. M. Goldberg, who was treating her for epilepsy. The good doctor was even more astonished when Rosa showed him that she did not have to touch what she was reading through her skin, and that she could even identify colours and shapes, as well as read newspaper headlines, when these were hidden beneath metal plates.

It was not long before Rosa Kuleshova was being examined and tested by scientists in Sverdlovsk (now Ekaterinburg), the regional capital, and then at Moscow. But all, unfortunately, did not end well. Many of the Moscow scientists were suspicious and hostile, and the stresses of big city life, which included a constant hounding by the press, brought about a fading of the provincial schoolteacher's powers. This in turn undermined her confidence, which prompted her first to guess, and then to cheat, in some of the experiments she took part in. The disgrace this caused led to a resumption of her epilepsy, with the result that she was happy to return to Nizhni Tagil and to a life of obscurity.

But subsequent investigations by various Soviet scientists have resulted in the discovery of other individuals with dermo-optical powers, and also the finding that such perception can be taught to ordinary people. Where the latter are concerned, it has been shown that the ability to recognize different colours is the first step in developing eyeless-sight, which is helped by the fact that each colour has a different 'feel'. Red, for example, can be identified by its warmth, roughness and stickiness, and by its heavily-grained quality, while light blue, the colour with which it is most easily contrasted, is cold, dense, slippery and small-grained. In one experiment conducted by Dr D. K. Gilev at Isham in the Urals, twenty-two secondary pupils were taught over a six-month period to identify all the colours of the spectrum, various mixtures of these, and black, white and grey, by touch alone. And in Nizhni Tagil, an almost totally blind man, Genady Grigoriev, has been taught to 'see' colours and shapes, and to read newsprint, with his fingertips.

But the question that still remains to be answered is whether eyeless-sight is a physical ability, perhaps deriving from the presence of hitherto unknown light-receptors in the skin, or is a variety of extra-sensory perception. If it turns out to be the latter it is certainly a form of clairvoyance. Indeed, because Rosa Kuleshova could identify colours and shapes that were covered by metal plates, it looks very much as though dermo-optical perception will turn out to be extra-sensory in nature.

Chapter 6
Precognition

'I was superstitious about dreams then, and am still; and Catherine had an unusual gloom in her aspect, that made me dread something from her which I might shape a prophecy, and foresee a dreadful catastrophe.'

Ellen Dean in *Wuthering Heights.*

Precognition is the knowledge of events, which could not be inferred or ordinarily anticipated, before they happen. Unlike prediction, which is generally dependent upon the interpretation of natural phenomena or that of the patterns made by manipulated objects like cards, dice and rune stones, precognitive insights happen spontaneously, coming into consciousness most frequently in the form of dreams, less often as psychic feelings or as visionary presentiments. Its partner, retrocognition, is the intuitive knowledge of events that have already happened. Both capacities, because they involve an apparent dislocation in time, are the most enigmatic of our psychic or extra-sensory abilities.

Mankind has always wanted to know what the future will bring, and in ancient times those who had the power of prophecy were believed to have received their gift from the gods. Yet it was always a dubious gift, one that invariably brought misery and death to its possessor. Thus Calchas, the priest of Apollo, whose prophecies both helped and gave confidence to the Greeks in their war against Troy, died of a broken heart when he met a seer more able than himself. While Cassandra, the second-sighted daughter of King Priam of Troy, was cursed by the fact that no-one believed her prophecies and lived to see her city sacked and her father and brothers brutally murdered.

In recent times, despite the wealth of historical and anecdotal evidence supporting the reality of precognition and retrocognition, there have been many attempts to demonstrate such powers scientifically. One such investigator, Dr Eugene Osty, whom we met in the last chapter, was to write: 'Twelve years of experiment with many metagnomic percipients and a considerable number of persons have given me absolute certainty that there are human beings who can foretell the future of other persons. I say the future of other persons, I do not say the future in general, which I have not verified personally.' He also noted that those psychics he investigated were not able to foresee what would happen to themselves. This reflects what was said about seers in ancient times.

But while few people possess marked precognitive powers, each of us has the ability to at least glimpse the future. This faculty is most commonly exercised in our dreams. And, as the following personal examples demonstrate, contrary to Dr Osty's findings, we can on occasion be shown coming events in our own lives.

On 7 March 1979, I dreamed that the singer Elton John was involved in some fraudulent scheme that required the construction of an upright, chimney-like tunnel. This was about six or eight feet in height, rectangular in cross-section and started some two feet above the ground. The idea was that Elton John would climb up the tunnel to gain access to the place where he would get the money, but as the tunnel ended in the air, it was difficult to understand how the 'fraud' could be accomplished. But before he was able to commit the crime he was arrested. He was sentenced to three years and three months in prison.

Two days later I flew to Athens, where I booked into the Marina Hotel in Omonia Square. In the bathroom of my room I discovered that there was a window with mottled glass. I opened it expecting to find that it gave a view outside, to the back of the building. But to my surprise it opened into a rectangular shaft running up between the floors of the hotel. As the only light entering the shaft came from my bathroom, one looked up it and down it into blackness, hence the visible part was of about the same length as the upright tunnel of my dream. It then struck me that in Canada, where I had been living for the previous ten years, a bathroom is commonly called a 'john' – and that 'Elton' is an almost exact anagram of 'hotel'. The significance of my room number then became evident: it was 303. But while my dream did seem to foretell the discovery of a strange shaft running up past my hotel bathroom, I was not able to determine what the notion of fraud in my dream referred to.

I thought the hotel rates were very reasonable!

On 12 September 1979, about two months after I returned from Greece, I dreamed that I was temporarily without accommodation and had gone to stay with two friends of mine, Phil and Kira, who gave me a large, sunlit room to use. Not long afterwards Kira began arranging our various appointments at the hospital for health check-ups. She wrote these on a calendar which had each month divided into small rectangles, one for each day. My first appointment was on 2 December. There were others for each of us in the following year.

At the time I was not registered with a doctor in England, but because I bought a car at the end of October it became necessary, for insurance purposes, to see one. However, because I then went away to first Glastonbury and then Hastings, I asked my mother to see if she could arrange for her doctor to put me on her list, and if she would, to give me an appointment. When I returned from Hastings – which was when, incidentally, Peter B. telephoned me from Chandlers Ford – my mother told me that not only had her doctor accepted me as a patient, but had given me an appointment on 3 December, the day after the date indicated in my dream. Yet when that day came, as I sat in the doctor's waiting room, I noticed that because I had forgotten to advance the hands of my watch by twenty-four hours at the end of November (which has thirty, not thirty-one days), the date it displayed was 2 December.

Similarly, on the morning of 12 February 1980, I dreamed that I was a passenger in a big, American-type car being driven by David Attenborough, the naturalist. I was sitting in the back seat, while another man sat beside Attenborough. We were driving through a part of Africa. Attenborough was in the process of showing us what had been done to save the lives of certain endangered species of animals.

That evening my girlfriend took me to see Tom Stoppard's play *Night and Day*, which was being performed at the Phoenix Theatre. It was set in Kambawe, a former British colony in Africa, and in one scene there was an actual jeep on stage, into which three of the male actors climbed and drove off. Because I had never dreamed about Africa before, at least as far as I can remember, and knew nothing about the subject matter of Tom Stoppard's play, I believe that I had somehow glimpsed its most striking scene in my dream.

These three examples illustrate the typical nature of precognitive dreams. They show that such dreams often, although not invariably, relate to trivial events; that they do so in a rather roundabout way; and that they frequently weave into the situation people and happenings that play no part in the actual occurrence. And significantly, they are only recognized as being precognitive when the event they foreshadow takes place.

Yet there are on record many dreams of a darker and more momentous nature. Suetonius, the Roman historian, wrote that on the night before he was assassinated, Julius Caesar dreamed that he soared up above the clouds to shake hands with Jupiter, while his wife Calpurnia dreamed that 'the gable ornament, resembling that of a temple, which had been one of the honours voted him by the Senate, collapsed, and there he lay stabbed in her arms'. And in 1865, a week before his assassination at the Ford Theatre, President Abraham Lincoln dreamed of his own death: 'There seemed to be a deathlike stillness about me . . . then I heard subdued sobs, as if a number of people were weeping. I thought I left my bed and wandered downstairs . . . There I met a sickening surprise. Before me was a catafalque on which rested a corpse in funeral vestments. Around it were stationed soldiers who were acting as guards; there was a throng of people, some gazing mournfully upon the corpse, whose face was covered, others weeping pitifully. "Who is dead in the White House?" I ask. "The President," came the reply. "He was killed by an assassin." '

In 1975 Mrs E. H., a correspondent in Montreal, wrote to tell me of a dream she had had which seemed to presage two injuries suffered by her son.

'In my dream I was walking down a suburban street and beside me was a young sparrow,' she said. 'He was dragging his left wing along the ground and I noticed that his left elbow was hurt and his wrist broken. The following day my eldest son came home from school because he had had an accident and hurt his elbow on his desk. That night he went to play hockey and broke his left wrist during the game.'

Two other correspondents informed me of dreams that they have had which presaged the deaths of their mothers. Mrs S. M. of Laval, Quebec, wrote:

'In my dream my mother was hospitalized, had an operation, suffered very much and died. It happened exactly the same way in real life . . . This frightened me very much as I lived 800 miles away at the time and I didn't know of her illness until after the operation.'

And Mrs E. F. of St Kevin, Quebec, told me:

'I dreamt my mother was sitting in a coffin, but she kept insisting she was not dead. Actually she was sitting up but no-one but myself could see or hear her. She kept begging me to tell them but there was no-one who would listen. In the fall of that same year my mother died very suddenly and alone.'

The study of dreams as important mental activities was initiated by Sigmund Freud (1856–1939), who realized that they could be useful tools in psychoanalysis. Research into sleep, the state that produces them, came later. It began with the 1953 publication of a paper titled 'Regularly Occurring Periods of Eye Mobility and Concomitant Phenomena', written by two scientists at the University of Chicago. One of them, Eugene Aserinsky, had noticed that sleeping babies went through periods when their eyeballs moved about rapidly, as though they were watching something of great interest. Later studies with sleeping adults showed Aserinsky and his colleague that if they were wakened during these Rapid Eye Movement (or REM) periods, dreams were invariably reported. Yet if the subjects were wakened between two REM periods, they would rarely say that they had been dreaming.

This early research revealed two basic types of sleep, orthodox (or non-REM) sleep and REM sleep. Infants were found to spend about half their sleeping hours in REM sleep, a proportion that decreases to about one-quarter by the time adulthood is reached. This means that for an adult who sleeps eight hours a night, two hours of this time are devoted to dreaming. But the dream period does not come in one block. Instead, the depth of our sleep constantly varies through the night, and REM sleep, when dreaming occurs, only happens when our sleep is shallowest, which explains why we often wake up either during or just after a dream.

When we first fall asleep its depth steadily deepens and our brain waves become correspondingly larger and slower, decreasing in frequency from about ten cycles per second to one to three cycles per second. On reaching the sleep trough, the deepest sleep level, our sleep then becomes steadily shallower, until about one and a half hours after falling asleep we are close to waking. This is when we enter the first REM period of the night. Our brain wave pattern becomes suddenly quicker and more irregular, our eyes move rapidly beneath our lids and, in men, the penis becomes erect. And we dream.

The first REM period lasts for about fifteen minutes. Then the sleep cycle repeats itself, although the subsequent REM periods become gradually longer.

Thus we have on average five dreams a night, thirty-five a week, or about 1,800 a year. And that, of course, is a lot of dreams. Their very number suggests that they are not just important, but essential, psychic activities. Indeed, it has been shown that when people are deprived of sleep they spend more time in REM or dream sleep when they next fall asleep, which indicates that they need to make good the dream loss that they have undergone.

'But,' you may protest, 'I never dream.' You are mistaken. You do dream, but what you don't do is remember your dreams. The only person tested who did not dream was a heavily-drugged psychopath. Hence you belong to that group of people who are termed, where dreams are concerned, *forgetters*. Those who do recall their dreams are known as *rememberers*. Yet very few people can remember all their dreams. It is usually only the last dream of the night that we remember either wholly or in part, or a dream that has been particularly dramatic or frightening.

But why do we dream? Nobody really knows the answer to this. Sigmund Freud believed that dreams allow us to act out our sexual and aggressive desires in a way that was both secret and safe, thereby allowing us to give some expression to our deep-seated urges and hostilities. More recently it has been suggested that dreams are a by-product of brain repair, and therefore have no psychological significance. But this seems to be taking things too far in the other direction. Probably dreams help us to live with our day-to-day problems and anxieties, enabling us to examine ourselves and our relationships in a way that is unclouded by consciously-held beliefs and preconceptions.

But some dreams, as we have seen, allow us to view the future, even though that view is murky and distorted. In all, probably about one to five per cent of our dreams are precognitive. But because we forget so many of our dreams, this means that we have to make a special effort to record and capture those that might presage the future. This is best done by keeping a dream diary. To do this you should go to sleep with a pad and pencil by your bedside, and then, as soon as you wake up, write down any dream or dreams that you recall. If you do this regularly it won't be long before you have an interesting collection of dreams for your perusal. And sooner or later you will net one that is precognitive.

One such dream reported to me by Mrs M. W. of Lakeside, Quebec, seemed to be warning her that her house was about to be burgled. She wrote: 'I dreamt someone was trying to get into my home through my bedroom window. Being unsuccessful they went to the front door and I

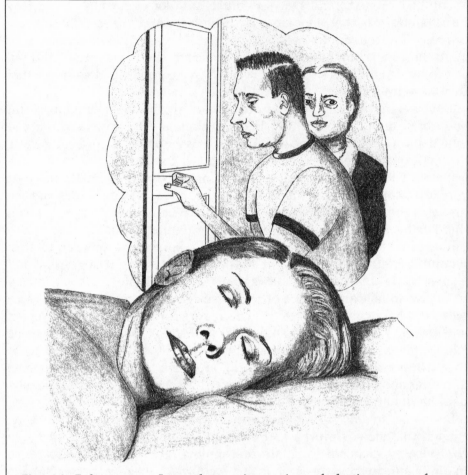

Figure 8: 'I dreamt . . . I saw them using a piece of plastic to try to force open the lock.'

saw them using a piece of plastic to try to force open the lock. I woke up covered in perspiration.'

But although the lady telephoned her sister to tell her about the dream 'in case anything happens because she is the type who always laughs at my dreams', she did not, as she might have done, take any special precautions. For as it turned out the dream was precognitive. Mrs W. was out for most of the next day 'arriving home at 4.30 p.m.

to find that my home had been broken into and robbed'.

A similar dream, although one presaging a much sadder event, was taken as a warning by the dreamer. Yet despite her efforts she was not able to prevent the occurrence she dreamed about from happening. The dream is taken from the Proceedings of the Society for Psychical Reseach, V, 322.

'Mrs Schweitzer dreamed that she saw her younger son, F., with a stranger on some cliffs. Her son suddenly slipped down the side of the cliff. She turned to the stranger and said, "May I ask you who you are and what is your name?" He replied, "My name is Henry Irvin." Mrs Schweitzer then said, "Do you mean Irving the actor?" and the stranger replied, "No, not exactly, but something after that style." On waking she was very worried by the dream and told her eldest son, begging him to recall his brother, who was away travelling for the firm on business. He ridiculed the matter, saying that F. was quite safe as he was in Manchester.

'About eight days later F. was killed on the cliffs at Scarborough, where he had gone for a week's holiday after completing his business in Manchester. Mrs Schweitzer, on visiting the place, met the man who had accompanied him on the occasion and recognized him as the stranger in her dream. She enquired if his name were Henry, and being told that it was, recounted her dream. He then said that he used to recite at concerts, etc., and was always introduced on such occasions as Henry Irvin, Jr. His real name was Deverell.'

Less frequently, but by no means uncommonly, we are apprised of the future while awake. This typically happens when some danger lies ahead, which we may be warned about by a strong feeling of unease or dread, by a voice, or by a vision of what is to be. It was a sense of alarm that Wolf Messing experienced three days before the earthquake levelled Ashkhabad, and which prompted him to leave the city beforehand. Here is another example of such a warning, which was told to me by Colonel Dawson in 1977 and who was kind enough to let me record it for later use. At the time of the incident he was an army captain stationed in a hill fort on the Khyber Pass in India, and was looking forward to taking a Christmas break in Peshawar.

'On Christmas Eve, 1924, I hailed a passing lorry that was going down the Khyber Pass, which was the usual way of transport, and got in with my suitcase and so on. But on the way down the pass I got a feeling that there was something wrong with the lorry, and I had a premonition that something disastrous might occur, so I asked the driver to stop and let me out. He didn't want to do so because while the Khyber Pass was safe enough in a car or lorry, one was not allowed to walk about. But I got out of the lorry and it went on. Luckily for me another truck came along a few minutes later and I got a lift with it. About a mile further on we discovered that the truck I had been in had fallen over the side of a ravine and was smashed to bits, and the occupants were lying either dead or dying in pools of blood. I spent Christmas Eve evacuating them to Peshawar and when I finally arrived at the club that evening was congratulated on my lucky escape.'

When a voice is heard it may either be an inner one, as in the following case, or it may appear to originate from some external point or source.

Captain A. B. MacGowan, an American army officer, while on leave in January 1887, had arranged to take his two sons to the theatre in Brooklyn, an outing they were looking forward to with some enthusiasm.

'But on the day of the proposed visit,' said Captain MacGowan, 'it seemed to me as if a voice within me was constantly saying, "Do not go to the theatre. Take the boys home, take the boys home." I could not keep these words out of my mind; they grew stronger and stronger and at noon I told my friends and the boys that we would not go to the theatre. My friends remonstrated with me, and said I was cruel to deprive the boys of a promised and unfamiliar pleasure to which they had looked forward, and I partly relented. But all afternoon the words kept repeating themselves and impressing themselves upon me. That evening, less than an hour before the doors opened, I insisted on the boys going to New York with me and spending the night at a hotel convenient to the railroad, by which we could start in the early morning. I felt ashamed of the feeling that impelled me to act thus, but there seemed no escape from it. That night the theatre was destroyed by fire with a loss of some three hundred lives.'

In eastern Canada, which was settled by large numbers of Celtic immigrants – Scottish, Irish and Welsh – and where there is a rich tradition of psychic and occult happenings, voices and other sounds that herald some future, usually tragic, event are known as forerunners. Hardly surprisingly, in view of the dangers that they frequently face, forerunners are often reported by sailors. This is what the Liverpool, Nova Scotia, seaman Captain Godfrey experienced, as recalled by his wife:

'My husband was in his bunk ready to go to sea when first thing a bundle of papers came flying across the room and hit him. He thought his mate was having some fun, but when he turned over he saw there was a blaze of fire the size of a man in the centre of the floor. A voice said, "Don't go in this ship or you'll be lost. If you don't go you'll live to be an old man and you'll die at home", so the next day he packed up and left the ship, but of course nobody knew why. They got a new captain and the ship sailed and was never heard of again. After that he sailed on ships all over the world and it was just as the voice said. When he died he was an old man, and he died at home in his bed.'

Premonitions are occasionally experienced by writers, who do not recognize them for what they are, but who, believing them to be the products of ordinary creative thought, incorporate them into the work they are writing. One interesting, yet little known, example of this appears in *Gulliver's Travels* (1726), when Swift says that the astronomers of Laputa had 'discovered two lesser stars or satellites which revolve about Mars'. At the time it was not known that Mars had any satellites or moons, but two were discovered by the American astronomer Asaph Hall in 1877, who named them after the two mythological sons of Mars, Phobos and Deimos. But perhaps even more incredible is the fact that the ancient Greeks accorded the virile, aggressive Mars (or Ares) – who was traditionally associated with the planet that bears his name – only two sons, whereas Jupiter and Saturn, whose planets are now known to respectively have thirteen and ten moons, were said to have fathered many. Could this be a case of an ancient intuitive awareness of astronomical facts?

Two remarkable instances of literary precognition were published in the late nineteenth century. Both presaged the same event, the sinking of the liner *Titanic* in 1912.

The first was authored by William T. Stead, the editor of the *Pall Mall Gazette*, who had a lifelong interest in automatic writing and spiritualism. The story appeared in the periodical *Review of Reviews* in 1892, and it described how a steamship collided with an iceberg in the Atlantic and sank. The only survivor of the wreck was picked up by a vessel that Stead named the *Majestic*. Oddly, there later was a ship of that name, whose captain, Edward Smith, was master of the *Titanic* on its ill-fated voyage. Hence the verse of Huddie Leadbetter's song:

> Captain Smith, when he got his load,
> You could've heard him holla, 'All aboard',
> Fare thee, Titanic, fare thee well.

Six years later, in 1898, the American writer Morgan Robertson, who claimed that he was inspired to write by a discarnate entity, had his book *Futility* published. This described how a supposedly unsinkable 70,000 ton liner, the *Titan*, set off one April to cross the Atlantic on its maiden voyage, equipped with insufficient lifeboats, only to strike an iceberg and sink, with the loss of most of her 2,500 passengers and crew.

As everybody now knows, the 'unsinkable' 66,000 ton liner *Titanic* was launched early in 1912, and in the April of that year began her maiden voyage to the United States, but struck an iceberg south of Newfoundland and sank. She was equipped with only twenty lifeboats, and this was the main reason why some three-quarters of the 2,224 people aboard drowned. Among the dead was William Stead himself, who ironically had taken passage on the doomed vessel, despite being warned by the famous palmist Cheiro that his life would be in danger if he travelled by sea, and by a psychic who had told him it would be dangerous to travel in April 1912.

Several potential crewmen and passengers decided against sailing on the *Titanic* because they had had premonitions that she would come to grief. One fireman who did depart with her, but who had a premonition of the coming disaster while aboard, took the opportunity to leave the ship when it put in at Cobh in County Cork, Ireland, before beginning the Atlantic crossing.

The Aberfan disaster of 21 October 1966, which happened when an avalanche of coal slag swept down onto the Welsh mining village, burying a school and killing 116 children and 28 adults, gave the London psychiatrist Dr J. C. Barker, who was in the middle of writing a book about premonitions, the opportunity of collecting data from those who had had foreknowledge of the event. In this he was helped by several newspapers that published appeals for such information. Barker either collected or received reports of sixty premonitions that appeared genuine and could be substantiated by witnesses. This led him to inaugurate the British Premonitions Bureau in January 1967, because he believed that the time had come 'to harness and utilize (premonitions) with a view to preventing future disasters'. A similar organization was founded in New York the following year. But although both have since received thousands of ostensible premonitions, only a very small percentage have come true, and none have proved helpful in the sense of saving human life and property.

Perhaps the most striking and touching of the Aberfan disaster

Figure 9: Eryl Mai Jones foresaw the Aberfan disaster in which she died

premonitions was that experienced by the nine-year-old girl Eryl Mai Jones, who was to die in the accident. The day before the mountain of coal slag moved, Eryl told her mother about a strange dream she had had that night. 'I dreamed I went to school and there was no school there,' she said. 'Something black had come down all over it.' And her mother recalled that two weeks previously Eryl had said to her: 'Mummy, I'm not afraid to die.' When asked why she talked about dying, Eryl again said, 'I'm not afraid to die' and added, 'I shall be with Peter and June.' The latter were children in her class who died with her, and with whom, four days later, she was laid to rest in a common grave.

The last type of precognitive experience that we shall consider is the vision, whereby a future happening is either witnessed as it will occur, when it is known as a veridical hallucination, or sufficient clues are glimpsed to suggest what lies ahead.

Where the second type of presentiment is concerned, the vision of a coffin, a corpse or a funeral procession is typically seen shortly before someone, who is usually a relative or a friend of the percipient, is about to die.

In her book *Bluenose Ghosts*, Helen Creighton recounts the vision seen by a woman resident of Annapolis Royal, Nova Scotia, who had recently had a baby:

'One night I was awakened from my sleep and saw a little white coffin in front of the bed. I woke my husband and said, "I'm afraid something's going to happen to my baby." He laughed at me, supposing I'd been dreaming. The next day for no reason my baby died in my arms.'

Another such happening, which was also recorded by Helen Creighton, was experienced by a woman who, after living for many years in the same house in Mahone Bay, Nova Scotia, moved to Lunenburg County:

'One night I knelt down to say my prayers and the house in Mahone Bay came up in front of me and, as I looked at it, I saw a funeral procession leave the house and go through the field. I thought a great deal about it, but didn't mention it to anybody. The house was then occupied by people named Evans. In the morning my father came in and said, "Evans' little girl died last night." I said, "What time?" He said, "Half past nine." I had taken note of the time and it was at half past nine that I had seen my vision.'

However, visions of the future do not always show unhappy events. For as Samuel Johnson noted: 'Good seems to have the same proportion in those visionary scenes, as it obtains in real life . . . that they should often see death is to be expected; because death is an event frequent and important. But they likewise see more pleasing incidents. A gentleman told me, that when he had once gone far from his own island, one of his labouring servants predicted his return, and described the livery of his attendant, which he had never worn at home; and which had been, without any previous design, occasionally given him.'

A good example of a veridical hallucination was seen by Air Marshall Sir Victor Goddard in 1935 whilst on a flight from Scotland. As he flew over the old Great War airport at Drem, which he knew to be in a derelict condition, he was startled to find that it appeared to be fully operational again. The hangers and runways had been repaired and four aircraft stood on the tarmac, one of which was a monoplane of a type unknown to him. All the planes were painted yellow, a colour not then in use by the RAF. Equally surprisingly, the mechanics who were working on the planes were clad in blue, rather than the standard brown, overalls. When Goddard reported this strange experience to his Wing Commander, he was advised to cut down on his drinking.

The Air Marshall realized that he had had a vision of the future when four years later, following the start of the Second World War, Drem was reopened as a flight training airport and monoplanes – coloured yellow – of the type he had seen were used for teaching purposes. And in the intervening period the colour of the dungarees worn by aircraft mechanics had been changed from brown to blue.

In type this vision is identical to that simultaneously experienced by two sisters living at Bridgeville, Nova Scotia, in the early years of the century. One night they were woken by the sound of a train. They scrambled excitedly from their beds and, rushing to the window, saw a train going by in the distance, where in reality there was no railway line. Because of this, they and their parents, to whom they related the vision, were not unduly surprised when track surveyors arrived the following year, and when, shortly afterwards, work was begun on a railway line that followed the same route as that taken by the train the sisters had seen.

But these accounts, while fascinating in themselves and certainly suggestive of the reality of precognition, are not wholly convincing to the scientist, who wants to be able to quantify and analyse the incidents and the faculties that allow their occurrence to be foreseen, which will enable him to formulate rules or laws governing the process involved. Thus it is not surprising to find that over the years various parapsychologists have attempted to investigate and measure precognition in the laboratory. But the results have not been either as clear-cut or as convincing as they would have liked.

In the early days of psychical research precognition was tested by having the subject try to predict what the order of a pack of Zener cards would be after it was shuffled. Once the subject had recorded his or her guesses, the cards were either shuffled by hand or, as happened later, by a mechanical randomizer. The predicted card order was then compared with that produced by the shuffling. Dr J. B. Rhine carried out many such tests with a variety of subjects and obtained statistically significant results suggestive of precognition. He also obtained positive results when he asked subjects to predict the fall of dice.

However, these experiments came in for criticism when it was recognized that the human mind could directly affect the environment, a capacity known as psychokinesis or PK. This meant that the results obtained in the precognition tests might have been produced by PK, that is, by the subject unconsciously making the mechanical randomizer sort the card pack into the order he desired or, where dice were employed, by causing them to fall as he had predicted. It was also possible that when the cards were shuffled by hand, the subject may have telepathically made the shuffler stop when he clairvoyantly 'saw' that the cards had arranged themselves into an order approximating to the one he had predicted, which would naturally have given him a statistically significant score.

It was to overcome these objections that some parapsychologists developed sophisticated machines whose operation was controlled by the decay of radioactive isotopes, whose activity is theoretically unpredictable. The leader in this field was Helmut Schmidt in the United States. He devised a machine known as a random event generator, which consisted of integrated circuits, an oscillator moving through its four positions at a rate of one million progressions per second and a Geiger-Müller tube that was struck by electrons emanating from a sample of strontium-90. The subject sat before a panel on which were set four unlit lamps, each provided with a push-button. When he had predicted which lamp would light if he pressed its button, he then did so. If his guess proved correct, the lamp lit; if not, it remained unlit. The machine automatically recorded his correct and incorrect guesses. Using this rather Heath-Robinson device Schmidt was able to claim that some of his subjects did possess the ability to predict which lamp would light to a statistically significant degree.

But unfortunately, Schmidt was later to investigate psychokinesis using a similar machine, wherein the emissions from strontium-90 controlled the alternate lighting of lamps arranged in a circle. The atomic decay operated a switching device which ensured that, when any one of the lamps was lit, there was a fifty per cent chance that the neighbouring lamp in a clockwise direction would next light, and a fifty per cent chance that the one lying in an anti-clockwise direction would light. Schmidt hoped to show that the subjects he tested would be able, by psychokinesis, to influence the lamps to light in a uniformly clockwise direction or, conversely, in a uniformly anti-clockwise direction. Indeed, some of his subjects were able to do this to a statistically significant extent, thereby demonstrating psychokinesis.

Yet this pulled the carpet out from under Schmidt's feet where his precognition results are concerned, because it was now possible to say that the subjects in the former experiment had manipulated the machine by

PK, causing the lamps they had predicted would light to light.

Hence while there is a wealth of anecdotal evidence supporting the notion that we possess the ability to foresee the future, it has proved very difficult to demonstrate this capability satisfactorily in the laboratory. Precognition therefore remains, from a scientific point of view, the most elusive of our extra-sensory faculties.

Retrocognition

'Retrocognition', like 'telepathy', is a term that was invented by the psychical researcher F. W. H. Myers, who defined it as 'knowledge of the past supernormally acquired, that is, not gained through the senses from records or from the memory of living persons'. It is also known as hindsight. Retrocognitive experiences have not been reported as often as precognitive ones nor have they attracted as much attention from paranormal investigators. This is probably because it is difficult to verify the events seen or felt, or to show that they have not in some way been created by the percipient's mind from material stored in his or her memory.

Interest in the phenomenon started with the publication of a book called *The Adventure* by Miss Morison and Miss Lamont in 1911. These two ladies, both Oxford dons, described how, while on a visit to Versailles near Paris, they had apparently seen a vision of the gardens as they had been in the eighteenth century, wherein bewigged gentlemen and ladies of grace and fashion sauntered about, whose laughter and conversion they heard, along with the music played by a small orchestra. The two dons were sufficiently startled by their experience to pay for the publication of their book.

What makes the incident doubly enigmatic is that they experienced it together. In this respect it resembles that undergone by two other English women in 1951, who, while walking along the beach at Dieppe, heard the 'sounds of cries and shouts and gunfire' which were followed, after a pause, by the noise made by what appeared to be attacking planes. Although nothing was seen which might have identified the past date of this ghostly attack, the two periods of auditory activity closely coincided with the two attack phases of the Dieppe invasion of 1942.

But lest it should be thought that such remarkable experiences only happen to Englishwomen in France, where romantic yearnings for action and adventure might have over-stimulated the imagination, it is worth quoting two further retrocognitive accounts.

The first happened to a married couple who were staying at an English country house, and who related it to Penelope Money-Coutte. She told the story to Ben Noakes, for inclusion in his book *I Saw a Ghost*. The pair, having gone to bed, were woken in the night 'by the sound of clanging bells and shouts of people, and they also heard wheels on gravel, so they quickly got out of bed and looked out of the window. They saw people with lanterns running about, and a large water cart, drawn by horses, come charging up the driveway.' The couple did not, as perhaps might have been expected, put on their dressing gowns and go down to find out what the trouble was, but instead returned to their bed and their sleep. The following morning, their hostess, after assuring them that nothing had happened in the night such as they described, suggested that they might have witnessed a re-enactment of the fight to put out a stable fire that had occurred one hundred years before.

An even more startling retrocognitive vision was seen in the early 1930s by Billy Ward, a commercial traveller for Rowntree's, who related it to my maternal grandfather Herbert Cole. Ward had been sent to a small town in Gloucestershire 'to pick up the threads of some dropped business', where he lodged at the Talbot Hotel in a room 'attached to, but outside, the hotel proper', wherein 'the oak beams and roof were black with age, the floor was of black oak with rugs here and there, the windows tall and narrow'.

'My host lighted a candle and bade me goodnight,' said Billy Ward, 'and I heard his footsteps grow fainter with a feeling of loneliness and of being cut off from the rest of the world. But within a few minutes I was undressed and in bed. I put out the candle and was soon fast asleep. I had had a long and tiring day, and whether my room was a tithe barn, a monks' refectory, or one in the hotel mattered not to me, provided the bed was comfortable, which it certainly was.

'The next I knew was that a terrific bang had awakened me, and I sat up with a jerk, my heart pounding wildly. There was a bright moon, and though it was not shining directly into the room there was sufficient light to see things quite distinctly. I remember glancing at my watch and noting the time, half-past one.

'From the further end of the room came whispering and cautious movements, and shadowy outlines could be seen against the further wall. Outside the noise was increasing: muffled voices, heavy steps, and the clink of metal could be heard.

'Suddenly a violent attack was made on the door. An axe was evidently being used. Louder and louder and faster and faster came the blows. I could hear the splintering of wood and the laboured breathing of the men who were striving to break in. As the door grew weaker under the assault and groaned on its hinges some of the shadowy figures at the further end of the room came forward and clustered quietly around it: and I could then see, as they were nearer to me, that they were all in helmets and breastplates. Some were richly dressed, and their hair hung in curls upon their shoulders.

'Crash! went one of the door boards, and a face was poked in through the aperture. One of the men inside the room made a vicious thrust at it with a pike. There was a scream and the face disappeared, followed by a storm of shouting and a redoubled attack on the door. All at once it gave way and fell inwards with a crash, and in poured several men, pushed forward by those behind. The broken door had now let in more light and I could see clearly that the attackers were similarly armed to those in the room, though of rougher appearance.

'The fight was now fully on and I was intensely interested. I was no longer afraid, but instead I felt exactly as if I was watching a "talkie". It was a glorious scrap. Backwards and forwards the parties swayed, and as the defenders were pushed back more men entered the room, until perhaps thirty or forty had crowded inside the door. The room was filled with shouts and groans, curses and invocations to the Deity, clash of steel upon steel, and thud of steel upon skulls. I saw one man's skull split to the chin with an axe. Dead men lay here and there and the wounded crept to the side of the room.

'One person I noticed particularly. He was tall and slight, richly dressed, with curling hair and a pale face. He took no part in the fight; in fact, I do not think he had even a sword in his hand. He remained at the further end of the room and in front of him was a ring of the tallest men of the party, who fought like fury whenever the attack pressed in their direction.

'And so the fight went on. Now the invaders were driven to the door; then with a rush the defenders were forced back to the other end of the room. The numbers of effective men on both sides were rapidly growing less, when all at once a shrill whistle blew. The invaders backed to the door, leaped down the steps, and disappeared.

'I awoke at half-past seven feeling like a wet rag, and after washing and shaving entered the hotel for breakfast. Inside the entrance hall I met the landlord.

' "Good morning, sir," he said. "Have you had a good night?"

' "No," I replied snappily, "about the worst I've had for months."

' "I'm sorry to hear that. The room is unusual I know, but the bed is one of the best we've got."

'Then I told him of my night's experience, to which he listened with a queer smile. "You are not the first who has had that experience," he said, when I had finished. "But let me tell you, you have dreamt nothing. You have had reconstructed something which actually happened in that very room between Cavaliers and Roundheads in the Civil War. I wish I could see it, but I can't, though I have slept in that room many times. The story which you have told me, however, is identical with what others who have slept there have told me.

' "The facts are these," he went on, "In the Civil War, Gloucester City alone stopped the Cavaliers' route of communication between Bristol and the North. It was so much a thorn in the scheme of their operations that King Charles himself came down to urge his army to take the city, and he made this town his headquarters. It was his room and his bed that you occupied. Gloucester was in a bad plight and on the point of surrender when the Earl of Essex came to its aid, and he made the first stroke to relieve it by clearing the Royalists out of this place. It is extremely probable that it was only a small party who knew of the enemy quartered here. Perhaps it was only chance which led to the attack, for it is certain that they never knew or guessed that the man in the background was Charles, King of England, or the result would have been entirely different. What you saw last night actually happened in August 1643, as all the records testify." '

The fact of precognition and retrocognition prompts doubts about what we call time. For while our common experience tells us that time is passing, with us growing older as it does so, our occasional ability to look into a future that apparently has not happened and back into the past that has, suggests that the past, present and future are not really as separate as they seem. In other words, time may merely be a mistaken impression.

If this seems outrageous, it is pertinent to remember that many mystics claim that time, space and the world of multiplicity are illusions. The ultimate reality is the Unity or One which exists in an Eternal Now. 'There is, then, one single epiphany,' said Ibn al-Arabi, 'which is multiple only by reason of the difference of forms by which it is received.'

It follows that in the Eternal Now everything exists and happens simultaneously: your birth, your life and your death are therefore happening together. That you appear to be placed at some point between the former and the latter only occurs because the view provided by your consciousness is a very narrow one. But when that view is enlarged, albeit temporarily, in our dreams and premonitory visions, this is when we see what we call the future or, retrocognitively, the past. Hence each life is, to itself, like a film that is projected, frame by frame, onto the screen of consciousness. The whole film has been made and printed: all we do is view each part consecutively.

Does this mean that everything is predestined? Yes, I'm afraid that, in a general sense, it does. And this is why those who have foreseen the future are unable to change it to their own advantage.

I'll leave you with the example of the astrologer Michael Scot (c. 1175–1232), who, mortified that his own horoscope revealed that he would be killed by a falling stone of no more than two ounces in weight, wore a steel helmet whenever he went outdoors. But one day in church, raising his helmet at the elevation of the host, a small piece of masonry fell from the ceiling onto his head . . .

Chapter 7
Scrying and Hypnotism

Scrying, which is derived from 'descry', meaning 'to catch sight of', is a form of divination that is popularly associated with crystal-gazing. It is a very ancient practice, whose origins are truly lost in the mists of time. Yet we do know that scrying was sufficiently widespread in fifth-century Ireland for its practitioners, who were known as *speculari*, to organize themselves into a guild.

The famous occultist Dr John Dee (1527–1608), who lived for the latter part of his life at Mortlake, besides the Thames, employed the services of a young scryer named Edward Kelley, who was able, by staring at the smooth, shiny surface of a flat piece of stone – his *speculum*, now preserved in the British Museum – to hold conversations with spirits and angels. From them Kelley dictated the Enochian Calls to Dr Dee.

More recently, the American psychic Jeane Dixon, whose predictions include the Communist takeover in China, the partition of India in 1947, and the assassination of both Robert Kennedy and Martin Luther King, has made frequent use of a crystal ball. And once she even employed an astronaut's tie-pin to prompt her prophetic utterances.

Indeed, scrying can be accomplished with any suitably shiny surface. This is why, at different times and in different parts of the world, scryers have used polished metal, stone and bone in lieu of a crystal ball or, more commonly, a bowl of water to which a few drops of black ink have been added.

From this it is evident that a crystal ball or other scrying device does not possess any mystical properties of its own. Rather, the shiny surface serves as a means of stimulating the psychic abilities of the viewer. It is, then, an ESP enhancer, which is why we must consider the practice of scrying in some detail.

You may be fortunate enough to possess, or have access to, a crystal ball, which are made in a range of sizes, the smallest having a diameter of about one inch, the largest being about eight inches across. If not, you can just as successfully concentrate your attention upon a clear piece of glass, a gemstone, a shiny metal object, or water in a glass dish.

For the beginner scrying is best practised alone. Your surroundings are also very important. The room in which you work should be quiet and warm, and you must be left undisturbed for at least an hour. In the old days, scrying was performed when the moon was waxing, preferably when it was almost full. The best scryers were believed to be virgins, whose purity supposedly contributed to their psychic revelations. But this was almost certainly a misunderstanding of the act of scrying, which most readily awakens the ESP faculties of the young rather than the old.

You may either work at a table, which is ideal if you use a crystal ball, this being stood on its stand on the table, with its black cloth beneath it, or seated in a comfortable chair, in which case you will hold the scrying device in your hands in your lap. In both cases the speculum should be positioned about eighteen inches from your eyes. The lighting of the room should be subdued so that any reflections in the ball, etc., are kept to a minimum.

Then, having made sure that the physical conditions are right, you can begin the process of activating your ESP.

At this point scrying appears much simpler than the practice of, say, astrology, palmistry and tarot card reading, which require the acquisition of certain esoteric facts and the understanding of various lines, symbols and markings, before they can be satisfactorily performed, while scrying, on the other hand, makes no such demands. But although scrying seems easier, it is actually much harder to achieve concrete results with it than it is with those other methods. This is because scrying requires you to activate and use faculties that are both mysterious and seldom called upon, or which may, in some people, be weak or entirely lacking.

The first step, once you are physically relaxed, is to dismiss from your mind all those day-to-day thoughts with which it is normally cluttered. Indeed, the secret of scrying is to still your conscious mind as far as possible, so that it becomes quiet, still and blank. While you won't find this easy, you will be helped by the fact that your eyes must be kept fixed on the smooth, shiny surface of your speculum. By focusing your attention on it you will gradually withdraw in a psychic sense from your surroundings. Little by little, you will cease to notice the table and other nearby objects, and faint sounds will not be heard.

This withdrawal is the start of an altered state of consciousness or ASC, similar to that precipitated by the Ganzfeld technique discussed in an earlier chapter. It is a condition in which psychic impressions are more likely to be registered. As the depth of withdrawal increases this is accompanied by certain visual changes. The crystal ball or other speculum may appear to grow cloudy or become apparently engulfed by a haze. Sparks of light may then be seen in the haze, or spots of light that were previously unnoticed may take on an insistent significance.

Many would-be scryers do not manage to proceed beyond this point, no matter how long they stare at the speculum. There are three main reasons for this. First, they may be psychologically unable or unwilling to fully activate their psychic faculties. Second, their mounting sense of excitement may push them back into normal consciousness. And third, a growing fearfulness of what their efforts may lead to seals off their minds to the production of psychic visions. Or they may not, of course, have actually reached a true altered state of consciousness, having confused what are in reality eye-focusing problems with the events described above.

The next stage is reached when the apparent haziness in or around the speculum disappears and is replaced by an inky blackness resembling a night sky. Then, into this blackness, grows a spot of light which, as it increases in size, develops into a visionary picture that includes a scene or scenes, figures and activity. Psychic images of this type take on one of two forms, just as dreams do. They may either represent present or future events veridically, or show them symbolically. The latter form of impression is far more difficult to understand because, like a dream of the same type, it requires interpreting. Conversely, instead of the blackness giving rise to a visionary scene, it may simply lead to a sense within yourself of what is happening or what will happen. Or, more rarely, a voice may be heard that gives you information.

However, you should not expect to have this final stage of the experience at your first attempt at scrying. Indeed, you would be very fortunate if you did. This is because the visions are the products of a deep altered state of consciousness, which can only be attained with practice. You may have to try several, or more probably many, times before you achieve it. The way *is* hard, for just as mystics have to meditate for years before they attain enlightenment, so you will have to work hard at scrying, even when you seem to be getting nowhere. In fact it is a technique that can only be developed and mastered by rigorous application, which is why there are so few talented scryers.

One does not, however, normally scry alone. Hence once you feel you can induce the trance state described above, you should start to work with another person, who will become the subject of your reading. Indeed, you are more likely to achieve 'transcendence' with someone else than alone, because the mind is often reluctant to work in a vacuum, so to speak, while it is stimulated by the presence of another consciousness. This is because scrying activates your telepathic, clairvoyant and precognitive faculties, which function best when they have someone upon whom they can be focused. In so doing, you will be able to obtain information directly from the person's mind, which will tell you about his or her worries or concerns, visualize persons and conditions that are important to him or her, and gain precognitive insights into his or her future.

Ideally, you should initially work with a friend who knows that you are trying to develop your scrying technique, and who can comment upon the impressions that you gain. This will help you to differentiate between genuine insights and those produced by conscious expectations. And you will also gain confidence when you learn that some of your impressions are correct, which will prompt further insights. Then, later, you can start to do readings for strangers.

This outline will hopefully convince you that scrying does not require you to wrap a scarf around your head or demand that your palm be crossed with silver. Crystal-gazing is not a mystical activity that necessitates a gypsy ancestry. It can be learned by most people, for it has more to do with the utilization of our ESP faculties than it does with magic and the occult.

The trance-like state induced by scrying is very similar to that created by the hypnotist, who may first ask his subject to stare at a bright, shiny object or at a light, while at the same time suggesting to him that he is becoming tired and sleepy. The subject is then told that his eyes will close and that, when he closes them, he will be unable to open them. The hypnotist may next slowly count or use some other verbal inducement to bring about a state of deep relaxation in his subject, wherein he becomes suggestible, which is known as hypnosis.

Hypnosis is a term that was suggested by the Scottish physician James Braid in 1843 for the phenomenon of 'nervous sleep' which he had been investigating. It was first accidentally induced by the Marquis de Puysegur and his brother Count Maximus de Puysegur, who were disciples of the celebrated Franz Mesmer, the magnetist. One day towards the end of the eighteenth century, the de Puysegur brothers were surprised to find that a shepherd boy, whose head they had been stroking with a magnet, fell into a trance-like sleep. When they were unable to wake him by shaking, the irritable Marquis ordered him to stand up, and the boy, although still in a trance, obediently did so. He also sat and walked when instructed to do so, and even more surprisingly could answer questions that were put to him. But what startled the de Puysegur brothers most was the boy's inability to remember what had happened to him when he eventually 'came out' of his odd trance. He had, of course, been hypnotized.

Since then, a great deal of research has been conducted into hypnosis, and although it is still not fully understood, its practical applications have been considerable. It has been successfully used to help people overcome phobias, stop smoking and ignore pain.

The unusual thing about hypnosis is that while it appears to be a genuine altered state of consciousness, it is not, like sleep and dreaming, accompanied by any observable bodily changes. For instance, the brain wave pattern and the pulse rate of a hypnotized person are identical to those of someone taking his ease in a chair.

While most people can be hypnotized if they co-operate with the hypnotist, the depth of trance varies from person to person. About five per cent of the population are deep-trance subjects. These are very suggestible. In one experiment some deep-trance subjects who had warts were told, while hypnotized, that the warts on the right side of their bodies would disappear. And in a few days those warts did indeed mysteriously vanish.

More recently it has been shown that our subjective appreciation of time can be accelerated when we are hypnotized. For example, when the New York researcher Jean Houston hypnotized piano students and then asked them to intensely visualize their practice session, she found that one minute of visualization produced the same benefit as sixty minutes of actual piano practice.

In 1975 Allan Lundell of McGill University did some similar experimentation. He compared the ability of people to recognize geometrical shapes in their normal, unhypnotized state with their capacity to do so while in a hypnotically time-distorted state. He began the

Figure 10: Allan Lundell and the complex shape-generating
computer PDP 11

experiment by training volunteers in time-distortion.

'I first hypnotize the subject,' Lundell told me while his research was
still in progress, 'then tell him to visualize, say, going into a store to buy
something. I get him to repeat the exercise several times and gradually
reduce the length of time that he has to do the task. In this way I teach
him to experience more events in a shorter period of time.'

Then, once this had been learned, the subject was asked to sit in front
of a computer screen and visualize a similar sequence as though it was
actually appearing on the screen like a film running at a fast speed.

'While he watches the visualization I superimpose one of ten complex
geometrical shapes on the screen line by line, each line disappearing
before the next appears,' explained Lundell. 'I then say "stop" and get him
to draw what he saw. I have him do this in a hypnotized and an
unhypnotized condition.'

Later, the two sets of ten drawings made by each volunteer were independently evaluated by four judges. The results showed that people do recognize shapes better in a time-distorted state. This suggests that the brain processes governing shape recognition are accelerated when a person is hypnotically time-distorting. Lundell believes that this may have a practical application.

'While hypnotic time-distortion might not help someone to learn a new concept more easily,' he said, 'it may facilitate certain types of learning such as speed reading, and stimulate creativity.'

Hypnosis has also been extensively investigated as a possible ESP enhancer. The best known researcher in this area is Dr Milan Ryzl, who, while still in his native Czechoslovakia, compared the clairvoyant and precognitive abilities of subjects in their normal, unhypnotized state with those exhibited when they were hypnotized. His results clearly showed that hypnotized subjects possess heightened extra-sensory perceptivity. However, not all researchers have obtained such positive results. For instance, Dr J. B. Rhine tested extra-sensory perception in hypnotized subjects but found that their scores were no better than those they obtained when they were unhypnotized. He therefore concluded that hypnosis did not stimulate ESP.

Such mixed results may mean that the success or failure of an experiment involving ESP depends as much as anything upon the attitude and expectations of the experimenter. Thus because Ryzl believed that hypnosis is an ESP enhancer, he obtained the results he anticipated, while Rhine, who presumably did not, could not do so. In fact those researchers who frequently get positive results in ESP testing have been called 'catalysts', whilst those who do not are termed 'inhibitors'. In this sense they are rather similar to the two types of subjects discovered by Dr Gertrude Schmeidler, the 'sheep' and the 'goats'.

Which all suggests that extra-sensory perception experimentation in particular is a true meeting of minds.

Chapter 8
The Oracles

The ancient Greeks, like their contemporaries of other nations, believed that human life is predestined. What happens to each of us, they said, is determined by the Moerae or three Fates, whom they named Clotho, Lachesis and Atropos. Clotho spun out each life as a thread, so determining by its start when we are born, and by its thickness, strength and the material from which it is made, our physical constitution, health and appearance, and the wealth, honours and success we may attain; Lachesis, by measuring the thread, ordained when we would die; and Atropos, by cutting the thread, both brought about our death and decided how we would die. Even the gods, some Greeks held, were subject to the Fates, although others believed that Zeus was the supreme arbiter of both man's and the gods' destiny. Yet as Homer indicated, the Greeks also thought, somewhat paradoxically, that anyone could, through his own folly, bring down worse happenings upon himself than the Fates had destined. Thus in Book 1 of the *Odyssey*, Homer has Zeus say:

> . . . O how falsely men
> Accuse us Gods as authors of their ill!
> When, by the bane their own bad lives instill,
> They suffer all the miseries of their states,
> Past our inflictions, and beyond their fates.

The Greeks likewise believed that because their many gods and goddesses knew what our fate is, they would, when consulted in the appropriate way, reveal it through their priests and priestesses. Such consultations took place at various sacred places known as oracles, each of which was dedicated to one of the deities or, as at some, to an oracular hero or heroine, such as Heracles and Pasiphae. The oracles were held in very high regard and were consulted by every rank and class of person, from the poorest to the most rich and powerful. The latter frequently hoped to curry favour with the deity concerned by giving gifts of money, gemstones and precious metals to the oracle through which he or she spoke, thereby adding to the wealth and grandeur of the oracle and increasing its prestige. And while a modern cynic might say that oracular consultation was superstition gone mad, the fact remains that many of the divinely-inspired pronouncements came true. This suggests that the priests and priestesses had precognitive powers and knew how to tap them.

The most famous of the ancient oracles was at Delphi, where the god Apollo supposedly revealed the future through specially trained priestesses called Pythia, whose name derived from the noxious serpent Python that Apollo killed there. That Delphi attained the eminence it did, to the extent that it was consulted by both Greeks and foreigners, was partly due to the magnificence of its setting and partly to the fact that Apollo was acknowledged as the god of prophecy. He was actually the most attractive of the Greek deities, not simply because he was believed to possess outstanding physical beauty, but because he was thought to inspire musical and artistic creativity. His title, Phoebus, meaning 'shining', linked him with the sun and, in turn, with light, brightness, health, openness, life and revelation.

Yet Apollo was not an indigenous Greek deity. His worship may have derived from Asia Minor or, as is more likely, from northern Europe. The Greeks claimed that he spent three months of every year away from Delphi, when he visited the Hyperboreans or 'people living beyond the north wind', which indicates a northern European connection. And Robert Graves thought that the name Apollo came from the root 'abol' meaning 'an apple', whose tree belongs to northern Europe rather than the south or east.

Delphi was founded in about 1100 BC when, according to myth, Apollo seized the site from the Great Goddess, Mother Earth, and made it his own. Tradition says that the first shrine was constructed of wax and feathers; the second, of twisted fern-stalks; the third, of laurel branches; the fourth, of bronze; the fifth, of dressed stone (this was destroyed by fire in 489 BC); and the sixth, made of marble, was the shrine that existed in classical antiquity, and to which, at later times, various additions were made.

Figure 11: Phoebus Apollo, the Lord of Light

The holiest place at Delphi was the oracular vault or *adyton*, situated in the basement of the temple. It was into this small, dark and cramped chamber that the Pythia descended to enter into mystical union with Apollo, accompanied by her male assistant and interpreter. The Pythia, of whom there were several at any one time and who prophesied on a rota system, was originally required to be a young virgin, but after one was raped by a farmer from Thessaly, women over the age of fifty were initiated into the role, dressed symbolically in girls' clothes.

To answer the question that was put to the god by the anxious enquirer, who may have been as wealthy and important as Croesus, king of Lydia, who first tested the oracle's accuracy before asking what the outcome would be if he made war against Persia, the Pythia would induce a prophetic trance by following an old and well-tried technique. This was based upon the hallucinogenic properties of bay leaves, a tree of the laurel family (namely *Laurus nobilis*), which was considered sacred to Apollo. At the Pythia's command, her assistant would burn chopped bay leaves, barley grains and hemp in the flame of an oil lamp, the smoke of which quickly filled the adyton and the Pythia's and her interpreter's lungs. Then, to add to the effect of these intoxicating fumes, the Pythia would chew some bay leaves, which introduced the potassium cyanide they contained into her blood via her stomach and small intestine. Care was needed at this stage because potasium cyanide is poisonous and an ingested excess would have put her into a coma, from which she might not have recovered. Having thereby achieved the desired level of ecstatic dissociation, whereby her precognitive faculties were activated, the Pythia would begin to intone her reply, haltingly, disjointedly and, almost certainly, ramblingly. As she spoke, her interpreter would record the chief points of what she said and this would be transformed into a readable poem or short piece of prose once the adyton had been quitted. And it was this completed work, the very words of the great god Apollo, that so often influenced the political, military and social life of the ancient world.

Hardly surprisingly, Apollo's answers were often difficult to understand, despite the help given to the client in their interpretation by another priestly assistant, the *exegetes Pythochrestos*, who tried to resolve the frequent ambiguities. Indeed, Apollo was called 'Loxias', which means 'the ambiguous'. For instance, to Croesus' question as to what would be the result if he attacked Persia, the oracle replied:

'Croesus, if you make war against the Persians you will humble a great empire; hence you are advised to discover which Greek state is the strongest and form an alliance with it.'

The Lydian king was greatly pleased with this answer, for which he had given the Delphic oracle gold ingots worth at today's prices about £50 million, and immediately made a pact of alliance with the Spartans, whom he ascertained were the most redoubtable of the Greeks. He then set about invading Persia. But unfortunately he did so with an army that was smaller than that of Cyrus, the Persian king, whose forces he engaged at Pteria, in Cappadocia, which is now part of eastern Turkey. The battle was long and bravely fought, but at the end of the day neither side had gained a victory. Thus when Cyrus did not attack him on the following day, Croesus decided to return to his capital of Sardis and enlarge his army by appealing for help from his allies, believing that Cyrus would not dare pursue him after so close a fight. In this he was wrong. Cyrus and his army followed swiftly after him, defeated his soldiers on the outskirts of Sardis and then besieged the city in which Croesus had taken refuge. The Lydian monarch sent desperate messages for help to his allies, yet before any of them could come to his aid Sardis was captured and Croesus taken prisoner. When he later complained to the oracle, Croesus was told that the fault was his own: he should have asked which empire was destined to be humbled.

Some six hundred years later, the Roman Emperor Nero, having lavished gifts of money on Delphi, also consulted the oracle with regard to his fate, and was told that he must beware of 'the seventy-third year'. He was likewise pleased by this answer, assuming that his reign was safe until he reached the age of seventy-three. But not long afterwards he was deposed in a revolt led by Servius Galba, who was then seventy-three years old. But the decadent Emperor should have been warned of his fate by a dream he had had, in which he found himself steering a ship, but whose tiller was torn from his hands. Nero killed himself in AD 68. He was thirty-two years old.

The oracle at Delphi continued to divine the future until the last quarter of the fourth century AD, when it was closed by the Christian Emperor Theodosius. It was demolished by his son Arcadius, who became Emperor of the Eastern Roman Empire in AD 395, and who, like his father, believed that the pagan gods were devils. His unreasonable prejudice brought almost fifteen hundred years of prediction by the priestesses of Apollo to an end.

Apollo had other oracles, although none was so well-regarded as Delphi. Different divinatory techniques were also employed. At Ismenium, Apollo's priests foretold the future from the entrails of slaughtered animals, while at Clarus the priests drank water from a sacred well before giving their oracular pronouncements. And at the god's shrine at Telmessus, dreams were interpreted.

Zeus, the king of the gods, had many oracular shrines, which is not surprising in view of his divine status. However, there were two oracles dedicated to him that rivalled Delphi in esteem. One of these, at Dodona in Epirus, was in Greece, the other, at Ammon, was in distant Libya. And both were, like Delphi, consulted by the wealthy, the famous and the powerful.

At Dodona, Zeus' will was primarily revealed by a large and sacred oak that grew at the site, and by the stream that sprang from its base. In fact, four separate divinatory techniques were employed by the priestesses, two dependent upon the wind, one upon the sound made by the babbling stream and one upon the cooing of doves. The most important method was the interpretation of the rustling sound made by the oak's leaves; and this was supplemented by the priestesses listening to the sound made by bronze vessels which were hung from its branches, clanking together. It is not known whether the enquirers had a choice of method or if the method was dictated by the weather conditions at the time. Perhaps on windy days the oak tree sounds were heeded, while on calm days the doves were listened to or, if the doves had flown away, the stream was consulted. In this way there would always have been some divine voice available for interpretation.

Herodotus tells us that Dodona was the most ancient oracle in Greece, which places its founding sometime before 1100 BC, and that both it and Ammon were selected as oracular sites by two black doves which had been released from Thebes in Egypt. One flew to Dodona, where it alighted on a branch of the aforementioned oak and announced, in a human voice, that an oracle dedicated to Zeus should be built there. The other made its way to Ammon, where it likewise told the startled oasis dwellers to found an oracle to Zeus, although it presumably perched on a palm tree and not an oak. The doves' instructions were carried out and the oracles subsequently grew and prospered.

The oracle at Ammon, no doubt because it was remote and difficult to get to, was considered to be infallible, although its priests failed to satisfy Croesus when he set them the same test as he had the Delphic Pythia. It had also been visited by two mythical heroes, which gave it prestige, as a visit there could be equated, in part, with their acts of bravery. The first of these, Perseus, consulted the oracle when he set out to slay the Gorgon Medusa, and the second, Heracles, did the same when he visited Libya after completing his eleventh labour, although Zeus was apparently reluctant to reveal the future to him. Arrian, in his *Life of Alexander the Great*, tells us that Alexander, eager to attain the same degree of fame as Perseus and Heracles, made a special visit to Ammon. There 'he put his

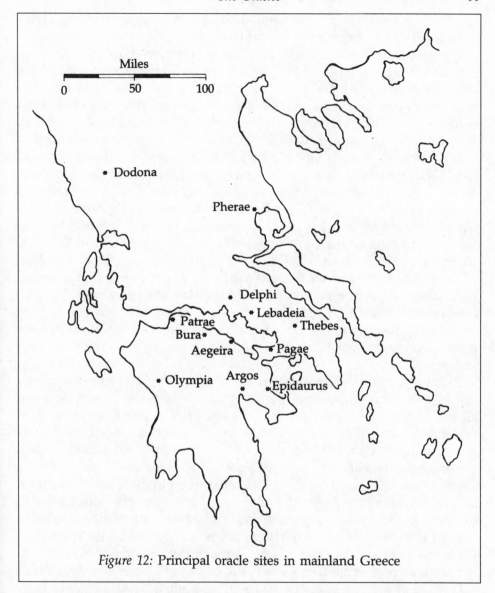

Figure 12: Principal oracle sites in mainland Greece

question to the oracle and received (or so he said) the answer which his heart desired'. We are not told what the question was, but it may well have been about his ancestry: was he, as he believed, a descendant of Zeus? If so, he was semi-divine, a demi-god. And indeed, many who knew him felt that he was a god. He died, like Nero, aged thirty-two, having conquered most of the known world.

The priests at Ammon used a divinatory method that was said to be similar to that employed at Delphi, which presumably means that they ate some form of chemical stimulant to heighten their ESP. But again, this was only one of several techniques employed by the priests at the shrines dedicated to Zeus. At Olympia, for example, which was founded not long after Dodona, the future was divined from the inspection of entrails.

At the oracles of other deities a variety of divinatory methods were also used. The priestesses at Aegeira, which was dedicated to Mother Earth, drank bull's blood before prophesying, which must have been as unpleasant as it sounds. At the oracle of Demeter, at Patrae in western Greece, the priestesses lowered a mirror into a sacred well and foretold the future from the patterns of light it reflected. And at Pherae in Thessaly, where there was an oracle dedicated to Hermes, the querents received the god's answer in the form of the first words they heard spoken by a passer-by as they left the market place. The Romans set great store by such randomly uttered remarks, to the extent that, when they were considering abandoning Rome after its destruction by the Gauls in 386 BC, they were persuaded to stay by the cry of an officer to his troops, who shouted: 'Let's stop here!'

The interpretation of dreams was of particular importance at the oracles of Asclepius, the son of Apollo and Coronis, whom the Greeks regarded as the founder of medicine. His shrines attracted the sick and were therefore among the busiest. Those visiting them did not expect to be miraculously healed, but hoped that the god would reveal to them in their dreams how their illness could be successfully treated. To prompt such dreams they fasted and then slept on the ground in the temple's precinct, and any dream or dreams that they had were reported the following morning to the priest or medical consultant to whom they had been assigned, who would help them with its or their interpretation. Asclepius's chief shrine was at Epidaurus at the foot of Mount Titthion, the second most important was on the island of Cos in the Aegean.

The use of dreams as an aid in the fight against disease has not been limited to ancient times. Both Freud and Jung believed that their interpretation could help with the resolution of psychological disorders, while Dr Vasili Kasatkin of Leningrad in the Soviet Union has shown that dreams can often warn of a health breakdown as much as a year before it happens. The latter, through a study of over 20,000 dreams, discovered that dreams which are repeated and unpleasant are usually the forerunners of a diseased condition, which the unconscious presumably knows about before the symptoms become evident. Kasatkin says, for example, that repeated dreams of a chest injury, such as being shot or knifed, signify either heart disease or an incipient heart attack, and that repeated dreams of a blow to the head, or a head injury, or even the wearing of a tight and uncomfortable hat, may reveal a future brain tumour or other brain disorder. His work suggests that anyone who has repeated dreams wherein a part of his body is injured, constricted, paralysed or otherwise prevented from moving normally, or if such a condition affects anyone else in his dreams, this should be taken as a warning of impending ill-health to the area in question, which should be thoroughly checked-out by a doctor. This will allow treatment to be started before the condition becomes obvious and perhaps more life-threatening.

Chapter 9
Psychokinesis

Late in 1974 I took part in a programme about fortune-telling at CFOX radio station in Montreal. After the show, while having a coffee, I spoke with a couple of the secretaries, who had been very interested in what they had heard. During our conversation, which moved from fortune-telling to other paranormal matters, I happened to mention psychokinesis, and, finding out that neither of them knew what it was, I went on to tell them that it was the ability of the mind to directly affect physical objects, by making them move or, as the Israeli Uri Geller had recently demonstrated on television, by bending or otherwise distorting them. As I described the bending of a key by mind power, I clearly pictured the bunch of keys that I had in my pocket and visualized the ignition key of my van bending. Oh yes! they cried, they had heard of that, and we went on to talk about other things. Then, later, having said my goodbyes, I went out to the CFOX car park, took out my keys and discovered, to my surprise, that the very key I had imagined bending was bent. I was fortunate that I could still start the vehicle with it, yet even more fortunate in having had a direct and very personal exhibition of what is now known as 'psychokinetic metal bending' or PKMB.

This does not mean, I must hasten to add, that I am a psychic metal bender. The above was a strictly one-off occurrence. I have not been able, despite many subsequent attempts, to bend another key or anything else by thinking about it, which is what Uri Geller can do so easily. This may be because, as many psychokinesis investigators have found, the phenomenon is often inhibited by consciously willing it to happen. For psychokinesis tends to occur, like most other paranormal phenomena, when one's mental state is positive but not too eager, approximating to R. H. Thouless' optimum psi mood of 'I want to succeed but I don't really care whether I do or not'. Because this is a psychological condition that is difficult to produce on demand, it makes psychokinesis experimentation particularly frustrating.

Psychokinesis ('mind-movement') or PK, a term which has largely replaced the older 'telekinesis' ('far-movement'), is not, like telepathy, clairvoyance and precognition, an extra-sensory perceptive ability, but rather a 'psi faculty'. This means that the mind, instead of perceiving or sensing things hidden in space or time, acts directly upon the environment, somewhat in the manner that a magnet can displace a compass needle or attract metal objects to it. And there is now plenty of evidence to suggest that psychokinesis is a genuine, if little understood, psychic ability.

But while psychokinesis only became widely known to the British public in 1973, when Uri Geller demonstrated his talent for bending keys on television, and, perhaps more surprisingly, initiated an outbreak of metal bending in the homes of many of those who watched him do so, it has been reported throughout history, although its manifestations were usually ascribed to the gods or to magic. However, Jesus' turning water into wine, his feeding of the five thousand and his walking upon the water of Lake Galilee are certainly instances of 'mind over matter' or psychokinesis. And many other strange happenings which were regarded as positive omens, like the fish that leapt from the sea and fell at the feet of the Emperor Augustus as he walked along the shore of Sicily, just before he was to fight an important naval battle, can perhaps be put down to the same cause.

In fact many of the phenomena witnessed at spiritualist séances, such as rappings, the levitation of tables and the appearance of apports, are now thought to be produced, not by the spirits of the departed or by downright fraud, but by the mind of the medium and perhaps those of his or her sitters. The first recorded example of such happenings, which was investigated by some of the best intellects of the time, took place in London in 1762. This was the now famous Cock Lane ghost, whose manifestations centred around a young girl named Fanny.

'The girl who knows by some secret when the ghost is to appear,' wrote Oliver Goldsmith, 'sometimes apprised the assistants of its intended visitation. It first begins to scratch, and then to answer questions, giving two knocks for a negative, and one for an affirmative. By this means it tells whether a watch, when held up, be white, blue, yellow or black; how

THE MYSTERY REVEALED;

CONTAINING

A SERIES OF TRANSACTIONS AND AUTHENTIC TESTIMONIALS

RESPECTING THE SUPPOSED

COCK-LANE GHOST;

WHICH HAVE HITHERTO BEEN CONCEALED FROM THE PUBLIC.

" Since none the living dare implead,
Arraign him in the person of the dead."
DRYDEN.

London :
Printed for W. Bristow, in St. Paul's Churchyard ;
And C. Ethrington, York.
1762.
[8vo, pp. 34.]

Figure 13: Title page of *The Mystery Revealed* by Oliver Goldsmith

THE MYSTERY REVEALED.

&c.

IT is somewhat remarkable, that the Reformation, which in other countries banished superstition, in England, seemed to increase the credulity of the vulgar. At a time, when Bacon was employed in restoring true philosophy, King James was endeavouring to strengthen our prejudices, both by his authority and writings. Scot, Glanville, and Coleman wrote and preached with the same design; and our judges, particularly sir Matthew Hale, gave some horrid proofs of their credulity.

Since that time arguments of this kind have been pretty much rejected by all but the lowest class. The vulgar have, indeed, upon several occasions, called for justice upon supposed criminals, and when denied, have often exercised it themselves; their accusations, however, in general fell upon the poor, the ignorant, the old, or the friendless, upon persons who were unable to resist, or who, because they knew no guilt, were incapable of making an immediate defence.

But of all accusations of this nature, few seem so extraordinary as that which has lately engrossed the attention of the public, and which is still carrying on at an house in Cock-lane, near Smithfield. The continuance of the noises, the numbers who have heard them, the perseverance of the girl, and the atrociousness of the murder which she pretends to detect, are circumstances that were never perhaps so favourably united for the carrying on of imposture before. The credulous are prejudiced by the child's apparent benevolence: her age and ignorance wipe off the imputation of her being able to deceive, and one or two more, who pretend actually to have seen the apparition, are ready to strengthen her evidence.

Upon these grounds, a man, otherwise of a fair character, as will shortly appear, is rendered odious to society, shunned by such as immediately take imputation for guilt, and made unhappy in his family, without having even in law a power of redress. Few characters more deserve compassion than one that is thus branded with crimes without an accuser, attacked in a manner, at once calculated to excite curiosity and spread defamation, and all without a power of legal vindication. If a person in such circumstances disregards calumny, and appears unconcerned, he is then accused of

Figure 14: First page of *The Mystery Revealed*

many clergymen are in the room, though in this sometimes mistaken; it evidently distinguishes white men from negroes, with several marks of sagacity; however, it is sometimes mistaken in questions of a private nature, when it deigns to answer them – for instance, the ghost (purportedly the deceased wife of Mr K.) was ignorant where she dined upon Mr K.'s marriage; how many of her relations were at church upon the same marriage; but particularly she called her father John instead of Thomas, a mistake indeed a little extraordinary in a ghost.'

From this it seems that when Fanny could see what the 'spirit' was asked about, the correct answer was given, whereas when she was ignorant of the correct answer, it was not, which indicates that she was responsible for the rappings. But as she was not detected in causing them deliberately, it looks as though she produced them, albeit unconsciously, by psychokinesis.

However, despite the great interest that the Cock Lane ghost aroused at the time, it turned out to be something of a nine days' wonder, and Fanny, visited as she was by men like Samuel Johnson, the Duke of York, Lord Hertford and Sir Robert Walpole, later vanished into obscurity.

This was not to happen when, in 1848, the denizens of the spirit world made their presence known to the Fox family of Arcadia, New York. For some weeks preceding 31 March, the family had been the victims of mysterious rapping noises which took place in their house. Then, on that evening, the two teenage Fox daughters asked the 'spirit' to repeat them when they snapped their fingers. The 'spirit' good humouredly obliged.

A few days later, when word of these events had spread, a group of neighbours assembled in the Fox home, and one of them, William Duesler, put some questions to the 'spirit' and received answers by a series of raps. In this way Duesler discovered that the entity was the wraith of a man who had been murdered and buried in the cellar of the house some years before. This led to the cellar floor being dug up and, quite incredibly, human remains were discovered.

This historic meeting between man and spirit, which took place in the same year that Karl Marx and Friedrich Engels published *The Communist Manifesto* and John Stuart Mill his *Political Economy*, caused a sensation. And the excitement grew when it was found that not only could the Fox sisters produce rappings in other people's homes, but that they were not unique in this ability. The spiritualist craze had begun. It was to continue for another fifty years, only to lose its steam when a number of investigators, some of whom belonged to the Society for Psychical Research, caught several famous mediums cheating. Their disclosures gave spiritualism a bad name, from which it has not yet recovered.

But by no means all spiritualist mediums were cheats. The most famous, Daniel Dunglas Home, was investigated on several occasions, and the effects he produced, which included the movement of objects at a distance, the levitation of tables and, on occasion, himself, and the materialization of a disembodied hand that shook those of the sitters, were both startling and apparently quite genuine. Indeed, Home's abilities in this sense have yet to be rivalled.

However, although such phenomena were ascribed by the mediums to the spirits, it now seems more likely that they were created psychokinetically by the mediums themselves. They did not know they were doing so, of course, but recent findings have shown that ordinary people can reproduce the effects of the séance room without having to call upon the departed for help. This is not to say that we do not survive death, but that those who pass on probably have better things to do than make objects move or dispense trite messages of condolence to those left behind.

Modern research into psychokinesis really began in the Soviet Union, when a woman with truly remarkable powers in that direction came to the attention of scientists in the early 1960s. Her name is Ninel Sergeyevna Kulagina. She was born in 1927 in Leningrad (now St Petersburg), where she lived throughout the Second World War, serving as she did as a tank radio officer and later on an armaments train, until she was almost blown to bits by an exploding shell. Yet she survived to become an apparently very ordinary, plump Russian housewife, whom one would pass in the street without a second glance.

But Ninel Kulagina was far from ordinary. Even as a young girl she was aware that she had psychic powers, which included the ability to 'see' what was hidden in people's pockets, and to 'know' which part or organ of a sick person's body was diseased. Yet it wasn't until she had a nervous breakdown in 1964, for which she required hospital treatment, that her psychic talents came under scientific scrutiny. And that only happened by chance. For while she was recuperating in a nursing home, Ninel passed her time sewing, and it was noticed by the doctors that she could reach into her work-basket and unerringly select the coloured thread she required without having to look for it. This led to her being tested by some Leningrad parapsychologists, who found that she did indeed possess, like

Rosa Kuleshova, 'finger-tip vision', or eyeless sight. This in turn resulted in a more serious investigation of her abilities by Dr Genady Segeyev, a scientist at the Utomskii Institute, the following year. He not only verified her eyeless-sight, but discovered that she was also a talented faith healer. She was particularly good at speeding up the healing of wounds, which she accomplished by placing her hands on either side of the cut or gash for a short period.

It was only later, having heard that objects often mysteriously moved and doors opened in her presence, that Dr Segeyev tested her psychokinetic abilities. He was astounded by what he found. For in a series of carefully controlled experiments, Ninel demonstrated that she could, by mental direction alone, move objects across a table, displace compass needles, and make a pile of matches explode outwards. She subsequently showed that she was likewise able, by PK, to separate the white of an egg, which had been broken into a saline solution, from its yolk, and stop the heart of a frog beating.

However, talented though she was, Ninel Kulagina's participation in these experiments was carried out at no small cost to herself. The concentrative effort required to move objects by PK accelerated her pulse to 200 beats per minute, dangerously raised her blood pressure and upset her EEG wave pattern, which are the type of physical changes that normally only occur when a person is suffering great stress. They left the Leningrad housewife exhausted, dizzy and depressed, and blurred her eyesight. They were to eventually result in a heart attack; this stopped her from taking part in further experiments. But fortunately, her talents were captured on film in the late 1960s, which remains as a valid and graphic testament to her psychokinetic powers.

Since Ninel Kulagina's enforced retirement from the psychical research scene, her place has been taken by a new psychokinesis star. This is Alla Vinogradova, the wife of Victor Adamenko, a parapsychologist working at the National Institute of Normal Physiology in Moscow. Alla became interested in psychokinesis after seeing the famous Kulagina film, and was to discover that she could also move objects by will power alone. And while, like her predecessor, she functions best on fine days, when she is in a good mood and not tired, and when she has not drunk any alcohol, she does not experience the same unpleasant side-effects afterwards. She needs to be close to the object to start it moving, but once this has been accomplished she can walk several feet away from it and still keep it in motion.

'I think only of the object and that it must move,' she told Henry Gris and William Dick, the authors of *The New Soviet Psychic Discoveries*. 'I concentrate on it. I must tune myself into the object. I feel as if some kind of energy is pouring from the sides of my fingertips, and from the sides of my hands.'

The best-known psychokinesis practitioner in the West is undoubtedly Uri Geller, whose metal-bending talents were discovered by Dr Andrija Puharich, when he watched the Israeli demonstrate them as part of his night-club act. Geller's powers are not expressed in the same way as are those of Ninel Kulagina and Alla Vinogradova. He cannot move objects by mental command, but he is highly effective at bending metal objects like keys and spoons, which he usually also has to stroke lightly. He can also start clocks and watches that have stopped, even to the extent of repairing those that are out of order.

Unfortunately, Geller has come in for a lot of criticism from stage magicians, who claim that his metal bending is nothing but a clever trick. Indeed, this has led to a widespread suspicion that they might be right. And yet Geller has been tested by several reputable scientists, some of whom have engaged professional magicians to watch out for trickery, and they have been satisfied that his psychokinetic abilities are genuine.

Uri Geller's 1973 television appearance in Britain resulted in the discovery of several people who could also bend metal by psychokinesis. While some of these 'mini-Gellers' were adults, most were children, who seem to be particularly adept at metal bending. Seven-year-old Mark Shelley, for example, almost ruined his mother's entire set of cutlery before deciding: 'It seems a waste of time going around the world like this. I'd rather play football for Ipswich.' Such youthful metal-benders were investigated by Professor J. B. Hasted, the head of the physics department at London's Birkbeck College, who was later to write in the *Journal of the Society for Psychical Research:* 'I therefore report my belief that I have been able to validate the metal-bending phenomenon on a number of occasions by visual witnessing, chart-recording, "impossible tasks" and the bending of brittle metals.'

Scratchings, rappings, the opening and shutting of doors and the movement of objects, some violently, have long been a feature of poltergeist hauntings. Indeed, poltergeists ('boisterous ghosts') are seldom seen, and their activity is often centred around an emotionally disturbed child or teenager. This indicates that the phenomenon, rather than being caused by an anguished departed person, is an expression of the young person's psychokinetic power. In this respect it is again relevant to note that the Cock Lane 'ghost' and the communicative 'spirit' in the Fox home were associated with young girls, whose reward for such disruption was an extraordinary amount of public attention. Thus psychokinesis, generated unconsciously in the mind of an emotionally disturbed child, may well be responsible for many so-called supernatural events, whose cause was formerly laid at the door of spirits, demons, black magicians and witches.

One unusual poltergeist haunting, which was investigated by the police, took place in Montreal in the summer of 1929. It affected a family living on St Famille Street.

The phenomenon began suddenly and unexpectedly. Mysterious knots were tied in clothing, curtains and bedsheets. And before long everything that could be knotted was tied into small, tight knots.

'I said to my boss, "That's a terrible thing",' one member of the family told me. 'And it was terrible. It put knots in everything. I wouldn't live in that house again for a million dollars. The spiritualists who came there said that somebody must have cast a spell on the place.'

When the knot-tying went on unabated, the family had the house blessed by two priests from nearby St Patrick's church. But the knot-tying continued.

The frightened family next called in the police. And when they detected a bad smell coming from the basement, it was feared that a murder victim might have been buried there – and its ghost had resorted to knot-tying in order to inform the living of its existence. But when the police dug in the basement they found nothing.

The police then performed an experiment that was simple but revealing. They placed unknotted handkerchiefs in one of the rooms and afterwards sealed it. When they later re-entered the room, they discovered that the handkerchiefs had been knotted. This established that the phenomenon was genuine. They next asked each member of the family to tie knots, and in this way found that those tied by the youngest child, a girl, were identical to those supposedly tied by the poltergeist. From this they concluded, probably quite correctly, that she had unconsciously tied the knots. And once that had been decided upon, the 'poltergeist' knot-tying ended as mysteriously as it had begun.

Experimental research into psychokinesis started in the nineteenth century, although the results obtained, while positive in the sense that they showed the mind could affect matter directly, lacked persuasive force because the subjects chosen were mainly spiritualist mediums, many of whose colleagues had been caught cheating to obtain the effects that they did. But when, in 1934, a youthful gambler told Dr J. B. Rhine that he could, when in a certain psychological state, influence the fall of dice, Rhine was sufficiently intrigued to investigate his claims. The results were positive, and this led Rhine to carry out further experiments with dice using student volunteers. Statistically significant results were again obtained, although as with his other ESP experiments a decline effect was noticed, the subjects doing better at the start of each experimental session than later on.

You may find it interesting, however, to test your own PK abilities using dice. A die has six numbered faces, which means that when it is thrown each number has a one-in-six chance of landing uppermost. Thus if a die is thrown a sufficiently large number of times, about one-sixth of the throws will turn up a 1, one-sixth a 2, one-sixth a 3, and so on. This implies that if you as the thrower can make a chosen number land uppermost more than one-sixth of the time by willing it to, a psychokinetic effect will have been demonstrated.

Start by sitting at a bare table with a die, a pencil and a notebook in which you can record your results. Select the die number that will be your target, which you want to land uppermost. Think of that number and, as you throw the die, will it to come up. Record the number that does land uppermost. Repeat the procedure at least sixty times and then analyse your scores. It follows from what was said above that if you find the number you selected came up more than one-sixth of the time, this indicates some degree of mental control. The result, however, would only be statistically significant if this happened when the die was thrown several hundred times, as it would be otherwise impossible to rule out chance as producing the bias. But if, on the other hand, you make the chosen number turn up twenty or thirty times out of sixty throws, then the odds against chance would be very high indeed.

A more interesting experiment can be done with two dice. This was devised by Dr Rhine, who made use of the fact that of the thirty-six possible combinations of two dice, fifteen give a total of more than seven. Indeed, the object of the experiment is to try to make the dice fall so that they produce a total of more than seven. So throw the dice together, willing them to do just that. Record the total you do obtain and then repeat the procedure as many times as you can. If you did this 144 times, more than 60 throws giving a total greater than seven, which could be predicted by chance, would be indicative of psychokinesis, although the dice would have to be thrown several hundred times before any positive results could be termed 'statistically significant'.

Testing for psychokinesis by dice throwing is a repetitive and boring business, which is why most parapsychologists have long since abandoned it. Yet Dr Rhine's positive results experimentally verified the genuineness of PK and led him to conclude that 'merely to repeat PK tests with the single object of finding more evidence of the PK effect itself should be an unthinkable waste of time'.

That, regretfully, is what many parapsychologists are still doing, forced by the criticism of their experimental technique by conservative scientists to contrive even more elaborate and foolproof methods, such as the use of random event generating machines controlled by radioactive decay, which were described in an earlier chapter.

However, one particularly interesting PK research technique has recently been formulated by Dr William E. Cox, a former associate of Dr Rhine at Duke University, where he invented many mechanical devices for testing PK. This is the so-called 'mini-lab', a sealed glass container enclosing a variety of small objects like dice, spoons, pieces of wire, pencils and paper, etc., that can be manipulated by PK, and which has allowed many spontaneous PK phenomena to be filmed.

The prototype mini-lab was the brainchild of the late Professor John Neirhardt, founder of the now-famous Society for Research into Rapport and Telekinesis (or SORRAT), a small group of Missourians who, in the late 1960s and early 1970s, were able to reproduce the phenomena of the séance room – rappings, temperature changes, table levitations and so on – by group psychokinesis. Dr Cox, a member of SORRAT, developed a smaller mini-lab that was made from a shallow, white-bottomed box with a glass lid, whose bottom was covered with coffee grounds on which was stood a pair of dice. This could be left anywhere in the home of a group member where it was out of the way. The task was to get one of the dice to move by PK, the trail that it left through the coffee grounds being

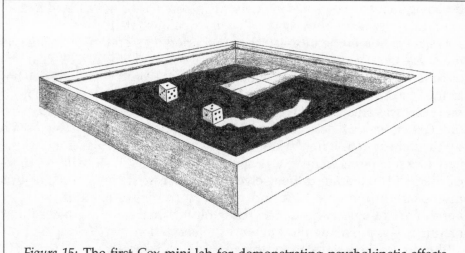

Figure 15: The first Cox mini-lab for demonstrating psychokinetic effects

evidence of its movement. This meant that the box did not have to be watched all the time. The second die was there to ensure that the box had not been tilted or shaken to produce the movement, the box's glass lid having been sealed to prevent direct handling of the dice.

These early Cox boxes were remarkably successful in demonstrating what has come to be known as 'spontaneous psychokinesis', that is, the production of PK effects which did not entail people sitting around and consciously willing one of the dice to move. The members of the group or family believed in PK and wanted it to happen, of course, and the movement of a die in the boxes showed that it could be generated without having to will it to do so. This made PK experimentation much less tedious and time-consuming than it had previously been, and this was probably an important factor in the technique's success.

The boxes were also sometimes set up without dice, so that the participants had to try and draw marks in the coffee grounds by psychokinesis. This also proved successful.

These successes led William Cox to develop a more sophisticated mini-lab, which consisted of an upturned fish tank stood on a wooden base and secured in place by steel bands and padlocks. A variety of target objects like pipe-cleaners, dice, leather rings, pieces of wire, coloured peas in a glass, some paper and a pen were placed inside the fish tank, which could, by being moved, deformed or twisted in some way, act as evidence of psychokinesis. And once again, PK was demonstrated.

The invention of the mini-lab took an important step forward when, at the suggestion of one of his friends, Cox set up lights and a film camera outside the fish tank, both of which were connected by special switches to the objects inside, which caused them to operate if any of the objects moved. It was an idea that was likewise successful, yielding as it did many film feet of psychokinetic movement that included a pen levitating, a pen writing on paper as if held by an invisible hand, leather rings interlocking and then separating again, paper spontaneously bursting into flame, pipe-cleaners twisting around themselves and, most mysterious of all, objects disappearing from the tank and then reappearing outside it, and the appearance of objects inside the fish tank that had not been placed in it originally – a phenomenon known as teleportation.

Should you be interested in doing so, you can also set up a Cox box in the manner described. And you do not have to buy a fish tank. A large glass jar will serve as a suitable container, in which can be placed several of the items mentioned above and then sealed. It should then be placed in a cupboard where it is out of the way, and examined every so often for evidence of PK. The only necessary prerequisite is for you and your family to believe in the possibility of PK and want it to happen.

In this manner you may be fortunate enough to have psychokinesis demonstrated in your own home, which will be far more convincing to you than reading about other people's successful PK experiments.

Chapter 10
Levitation

The levitation of objects, whereby they seemingly rise up into the air of their own accord and float, has occasionally been reported in séance rooms and during PK experiments. Even more dramatic is the levitation of people. And while this phenomenon is popularly associated with Indian fakirs and meditators, there are many accounts of it happening in the West. In fact, over two hundred saints and holy men and women who have levitated are on record, a list that includes St Francis of Assisi, St Thomas Aquinas, St Peter of Alcantara, St Alphonus Rodriquez, St Peter Claver, St Teresa of Avila, St Gertrude Salandri and, best known of all, St Joseph of Cupertino. This in itself indicates that a person can, through perhaps unconsciously expressed psychokinesis, defy gravity.

The term 'levitation' derives from the Latin root *levis*, meaning 'lightness', whose opposite is *gravis*, meaning 'heaviness' or 'weight'. Yet while some levitators report that they actually felt physically lighter when they rose into the air, others say that their elevation seemed to result from their being lifted as if by invisible hands. However, not all holy men have regarded levitation as being an act of God, despite its miraculous nature; some have thought instead that it was caused by the Devil. Indeed, the fact that Jesus himself walked upon water notwithstanding, the fourth-century Christian ascetic Pachomius said of a monk who had claimed to have done likewise, 'He is able to pass over the river as one who travelleth over dry land through the neglect of God, and the Calumniator [i.e. the Devil] helpeth him,' adding, 'I devote all my strivings, and all my anxious care, not that I may pass over the river by walking on the waters thereof, but in trying to flee from the judgement of God, and to escape, by the might of the Lord, from such Satanic wiles as these.'

Jesus' walking upon the water of the Sea of Galilee, recorded by St

Matthew, St Mark and St John, is not usually regarded as an example of levitation, although it clearly is, as without becoming lighter or being supernaturally supported, he would not have been able to do so. St Matthew says that when the disciples, who were in a boat, saw him walking on the storm-tossed sea, 'They were troubled, saying, It is a spirit; and they cried out for fear. But straightway Jesus spake unto them, saying, Be of good cheer; it is I; be not afraid.' And then, equally remarkably, St Matthew adds, 'And Peter answered him and said, Lord, if it be thou, bid me come unto thee on the water. And he said, Come. And when Peter was come down out of the ship, he walked on the water, to go to Jesus. But when he saw the wind boisterous, he was afraid; and beginning to sink, he cried, saying, Lord, save me. And immediately Jesus stretched forth his hand, and caught him, and said unto him, O thou of little faith, wherefore didst thou doubt?'

It is unfortunate that neither St Mark nor St John mention that Peter also walked upon the water, yet the testimony of the three apostles makes it clear that Jesus did. Jesus of course performed many other miracles or supernatural acts, such as healing the sick, raising the dead, turning water into wine and feeding the five thousand with nothing more than five loaves and two fishes, and said that all of us could do the same. 'If you have faith, and doubt not,' he told the disciples, '. . . ye shall say unto this mountain, Be thou removed, and be thou cast into the sea; it shall be done. And all things, whatsoever ye shall ask in prayer, believing, ye shall receive.' This is something that all would-be levitators should take note of.

Nonetheless, it is evident that the uplifting of those saints who levitated came about not by them seeking it or wishing for it to happen, but as a product of the mystical state known as *ecstasy* into which they sometimes fell. Ecstasy or rapture, according to those who have experienced it, is a transcendental condition, wherein the person concerned is filled with divine love. 'It comes, in general, as a shock, quick and sharp,' wrote St Teresa in her autobiography, 'before you can collect your thoughts, or help yourself in any way, and you see and feel it as a cloud, or as a strong eagle rising upwards and carrying you away on its wings.'

Ecstasy may occur as a result of meditation or prayer, or by prolonged contemplation of the divine or, in those who are particularly susceptible to it, as was St Joseph of Cupertino, by the mere sight of a holy statue or a religious relic. St Teresa frequently experienced rapture when attending church, where she tried to stop it from happening, apparently with little success. 'At other times,' she tells us, 'it was impossible to resist at all; my soul was carried away, and almost always my head with it – I had no power over it – and now and then the whole body as well, *so that it was lifted up from the ground* [my italics].'

Interestingly, St Teresa reported both an apparent uplifting of her body from below, which pushed it, as it were, into the air, and a feeling of physical lightness:

'It seemed to me, when I tried to make some resistance, as if a great force beneath my feet lifted me up . . . I confess that it threw me into great fear, very great indeed at first; for in seeing one's body thus lifted up from the earth, though the spirit draws it upwards after itself (and that with great sweetness, if unresisted), the senses are not lost; at least I was so much myself as to be able to see that I was being lifted up . . . After the rapture was over, I have to say that my body seemed frequently to be buoyant, as if all weight had departed from it, so much so that now and then I scarcely knew that my feet touched the ground.'

St Teresa's frequent levitations, while not happening much in public, were witnessed on occasions by those who swore on oath, at later depositions, of having seen them take place. Sister Anne of the Incarnation at Segovia was one who saw St Teresa levitate in broad daylight whilst in church. 'As I was looking on,' said Sister Anne, 'she was raised about half a yard from the ground without her feet touching it. At this I was terrified and she, for her part, was trembling all over. So I moved to where she was and put my hands under her feet, over which I remained weeping for something like half an hour while the ecstasy lasted. Then suddenly she sank down and rested on her feet.'

Most levitators have risen only a few inches from the ground, while others, like St Teresa, have ascended to a height of eighteen inches or even three feet. Yet considerably greater elevations have been recorded. St Peter of Alcantara, for example, is said to have levitated to a height of 15 feet, and the nun Sister Maria Villani to a height of about 30 feet. St Joseph of Cupertino may have risen even higher, as it is reported that on occasions he floated upwards to the height of trees.

Likewise, whereas some levitators have simply hung in the air, others have moved laterally as well, often considerable distances. The length of time they have remained aerially suspended also varies, ranging from levitations of a few minutes to those lasting up to two hours. Writing of one of her own levitations, Sister Maria Villani says, 'I felt myself seized and ravished out of my senses, and that so powerfully that I found myself lifted up completely by the very soles of my feet . . . At first I felt much fear, but afterwards I remained in the greatest possible contentment and joy of spirit. Though I was quite beside myself, still, in spite of that, I knew that I was raised some distance above the earth, *my whole body being suspended for a considerable space of time* [my italics].'

St Joseph of Cupertino, whose levitations are both astounding and well-documented, was born plain Joseph Desa at the village of that name, which lies between Brindisi and Otranto in Italy, on 17 June 1603, the son of poor parents, his father being a carpenter. He was a weak, sickly infant, unloved and unwanted by his mother, who grew into a slow-witted, clumsy, forgetful and generally ill-favoured child, whose habit of walking around with his mouth open brought him the nick-name of 'Gaper'. Yet despite his low-intellect and unprepossessing appearance, young Joseph was blessed with a sweet and friendly disposition, and was distinguished by a remarkable piety.

When he reached adolescence his mother had him apprenticed to a shoemaker, but his lack of co-ordination made him unsuitable for the trade and he gave it up. Thus at seventeen, in 1620, he followed his natural inclinations and asked a group of Conventual friars if they would admit him into their order. They examined him, were unimpressed by what they found and refused. He then successfully applied for entry into the Capuchin order, but his stay with them only lasted eight months. His slowness and clumsiness, and the fact that he seemed to be lost in another world, led to his dismissal.

Upon next being rebuffed by a wealthy uncle, to whom he had appealed for assistance, Joseph returned home. This led his mother, desperate to get him off her hands, to ask her brother, a Conventual Franciscan, to use his influence in having him accepted by the order. The brother obliged, with the result that Joseph was taken on as a stable lad by the friars at La Grotella. It was work that he both enjoyed and could handle, and his position was secure, if menial.

However, his personal qualities soon brought Joseph to the attention of his superiors, who decided in 1625 that he should be allowed to train for holy orders. The training period lasted for three years, but his academic progress was so slow that it was doubted whether he could pass the examinations. Yet he did so by two extraordinary pieces of luck. At the intermediate examination, during which the students were asked to discourse upon a Biblical fragment chosen at random from the Gospels, the bishop selected the one phrase – 'Blessed be the womb that bore thee' – that Joseph could talk about at any length. And when the final examinations were held, the first batch of students so impressed the examiners that they passed the remainder, which included Joseph, without further ado. The academic clod had become a priest.

The young initiate was to remain at La Grotella for a further eleven years, until 1639, and it was during this period that he levitated some seventy times. Each was usually preceded by Joseph going into an ecstatic trance, which itself was precipitated by him saying Mass or seeing a holy statue, whereupon he rose several feet from the ground to float, unsuspended, in the air. He once levitated having gathered a lamb into his arms, being 'lost in contemplation of the spotless Lamb of God', and on another when, noticing that his brothers were having difficulty in erecting the central cross of a calvary they were constructing, he floated some seventy yards from the door of the friary to the cross, which he effortlessly picked up and placed in the hole that had been dug for it.

These levitations, incredible though they were, were not the only signs of Joseph's holiness, for he was also able to heal the sick and was possessed of a strange power over animals, which led to him being compared to St Francis of Assisi.

Such marvels, however, did not pass without adverse comment and criticism, and there were those amongst Joseph's brothers who were embarrassed by and perhaps jealous of his miraculous gifts. This resulted in certain restrictions being placed upon him. He was not allowed, for instance, to celebrate Mass, for fear that he might suddenly float skywards, or to take part in any public function.

More serious concern was generated by the marvelling crowds that Joseph drew while on a visit to Bari province, and this led to him being summoned to Rome to be examined by pope Urban VIII, who was favourably impressed when he went into an ecstatic trance upon seeing him. The pontiff decided that he should be sent to the monastery at Assisi, but on arriving there Joseph temporarily lost his spiritual powers and suffered certain temptations which, though resisted, threw him into a severe depression. Hearing of this, the Pope again summoned him to Rome and it was during the journey there that his spiritual ecstasies returned.

It was when Joseph went back to Assisi that his levitations were witnessed by many eminent and influential people. For example, after being visited in his cell by the High Admiral of Castile, he was told to go into the church and speak with his wife, who likewise wished to see him. On entering the church Joseph caught sight of a statue of the Virgin Mary, which prompted him to fly 'about a dozen paces over the heads of those present to the foot of the statue. Then after paying homage there for some short space and uttering his customary shrill cry he flew back again and straightway returned to his cell, leaving the admiral, his wife and the large company which attended them speechless with astonishment.'

But notwithstanding these miraculous levitations, and for reasons that are still not known, the Inquisition of Perugia in 1653 ordered that Joseph be sent to the isolated friary at Pietrarossa. However, once news of the transfer became public knowledge, it was besieged by pilgrims. This was to result in Joseph being moved from place to place by the Church authorities until 1657, when he was finally allowed to settle at Osimo. It was there that on one occasion he carried a fellow friar up into the air. He remained at Osimo until his death in 1663.

A cardinal once asked Joseph what those in ecstasy saw in their raptures. He answered: 'They feel as though they were taken into a wonderful gallery, shining with never-ending beauty, where in a glass, with a single look, they apprehend the marvellous vision which God pleases to show them.'

Joseph Desa was canonized in 1767.

But levitation, though long associated with the saintly, is by no means only experienced by them. There are numerous accounts of it happening to ordinary folk, as well as to mediums and other spiritualists. Among the latter, the names of Daniel Dunglas Home, Eusapia Palladino, Stainton Moses and Carlo Mirabelli are the best known. Indeed, the levitations of Home, the most celebrated nineteenth-century medium, were numerous and well-attested, comparable in many ways to those of St Joseph of Cupertino.

Home's first levitation took place at a house in Manchester on 8 August 1852, when it was observed by several reliable witnesses, one of whom gave this account of it:

'Suddenly and without any expectation on the part of the company, Mr Home was taken up into the air. I had hold of his hand at the time, and I felt his feet – they were lifted a foot from the floor. He palpitated from head to foot with the contending emotions of joy and fear which choked his utterance. Again and again he was taken up from the floor, and the third time he was carried to the ceiling of the apartment . . . I felt the distance from the soles of his boots to the floor, and it was nearly three feet.'

On one occasion Home was reported to have floated out from the window of a fifth-floor room, below which was a drop of eighty feet, and to have re-entered the building by floating in through a window of the next room. This famous occurrence, however, has been the subject of much dispute, with some claiming that the witnesses hallucinated the whole performance, while Houdini denigrated it as a trick which he himself could duplicate, although he never actually did so.

It is interesting to compare Home's own account of his aerial ascents with those mentioned earlier. He wrote:

'During these elevations or levitations I usually experience no particular sensation other than what I could only describe as an electrical fullness about the feet. I feel no hands supporting me, and since the first time I have never felt fear, though if I had fallen from the ceiling of some of the rooms in which I have been raised, I could not have escaped serious injury.'

But while these cases are sufficient to persuade us that people can levitate, they do not explain how it happens. As mentioned earlier, the experience of the event also differs: some say that they felt physically lighter while levitating, some that they felt as if they were pushed or lifted up into the air, or both, while others, like Home, report that no such apparent external uplift was applied to them. Yet it is reasonable to suppose that if the mind can impress itself upon external objects to the extent to being able to move them or even support them in mid-air, which we have described as psychokinesis, then there is no reason why it should not also be able to similarly support the body in which it resides. How it does this is another matter. It may be that the mind is able to somehow negate the force of gravity, which would necessarily lead to a rising of its owner into the air, although it would not explain how he (or she) could prevent himself from floating upwards to an ever-increasing height, whereas as we have seen most levitators rise but a short distance to hang unsuspended in the air.

Levitation therefore remains a mystery, a very wonderful and marvellous mystery, whose explanation may lie more in the realm of physics than in parapsychology.

Chapter 11
Animal ESP

From time to time a story appears in the popular press about a household pet, usually a cat or a dog, which has been left behind when its owner moves house, only to turn up at the new and distant abode days, weeks or sometimes months later, having apparently found its way there by psychic means. Indeed, this remarkable locating ability has been called 'psi-trailing' and naturally suggests that we humans are not the only species to be blessed with ESP.

What then is known about animal extra-sensory perception? The short answer to this is, not a lot. There are many millions of other animal types on this planet, and while it is possible that all or many of them might have extra-sensory talents, what experimentation that has been done has largely been limited to those animals that are closest to us and are fellow mammals.

Such work dates back to 1920, when the eminent Soviet reflexologist V. M. Bekhterev, who worked at the Leningrad Institute for Brain Research, decided to test the claim of the circus entertainer Vladimir Durov that his dogs obeyed his mental commands. Bekhterev was suitably impressed when, having made sure that the dogs were not responding to visual clues, he found that they also obeyed *his* mental orders. The animals apparently could pick up telepathic messages.

But if some animals were able to receive telepathic messages from a human, did this mean that they could also communicate with each other psychically? The answer to this is yes, as was demonstrated by another, and rather gruesome, Soviet experiment carried out at the Novosibirsk Medical Institute by Dr Sergey Sperunski in 1974. He reared 500 white mice together, which he then divided into two halves. He took one group to the basement of the building and the other to the third floor. Then, while he observed the behaviour of those on the third floor, he had the mice in the basement killed. From his observations Sperunski was to conclude: 'Some type of telepathic communication took place between the two groups. During the trauma of death, a telepathic message flashed a warning of danger to the group that was not scheduled to die, causing fear and anxiety among them.' A similar telepathic signal was detected when an American researcher, again in the 1970s, killed the young of a female rabbit, from which she was separated by a distance of many miles. By monitoring the physiological reactions of the rabbit it was noted that her body showed signs of acute stress at the same time that her offspring died.

Dr J. B. Rhine carried out a series of experiments at Duke University, which he began in 1950, to test the paranormal abilities of cats, dogs and horses. He was able to show, where the first two animal types are concerned, that they could foretell when their owner would arrive home unexpectedly (by presumably picking up a telepathic message from him or her), anticipate when some danger threatened either them or their owner (possibly precognition), make their way home after being lost several miles away, and 'psi-trail', that is, find their owner at a place where they had never been before.

However, it has since been shown that cats, dogs and horses have both a very good sense of direction and an excellent memory, which probably means that they use ordinary cognitive functions to orientate themselves and make their way back home after being released some distance away from it. Thus if an animal is allowed to view its surroundings as it is being transported to the distant site, it can usually get back home again. But this is seldom the case if it is not allowed to pick up visual clues while in transit. Horses are particularly good at 'mapping' a landscape through which they are being led or ridden, which is not surprising when one considers that they see it from a superior height with eyes that are particularly acute. Dogs, however, have poorer vision than either horses or cats, and see their surroundings, as do cats, from a low altitude and in a rather drab monotone.

In the late 1950s Dr Rhine conducted an interesting experiment at Richmond, Virginia, with a three-year-old horse named Lady, which revealed that the horse, like Vladimir Durov's dogs, obeyed telepathic commands. Mrs Claudia Fonda, Lady's owner, had taught the animal to both spell words and add and subtract numbers by touching its nose to blocks on which letters of the alphabet and numbers had been painted. It would do this to spoken commands or, as Mrs Fonda claimed, to those that were issued telepathically. Having first made sure that Lady was not being given visual clues by Mrs Fonda, Dr Rhine had her mentally instruct the horse to either nose out a number or spell out a word, which it did with a high degree of success. Dr Rhine completed the experiment, as V. M. Bekhterev had done, by generating the telepathic commands himself. The positive results he achieved convinced him that Lady both received and responded to such telepathically issued orders.

When Dr Rhine later discovered a dog that had been trained to answer verbal questions by pawing its owner's arm the requisite number of times, it gave him the opportunity to test the animal's clairvoyant ability. The dog in question was Chris, the Wonder Dog, owned by George Wood. For the experiment, Rhine had Wood teach Chris to paw the ground when shown one or other of the Zener card symbols, once for a circle, twice for a cross, etc. He then put each card of a Zener deck into an opaque envelope, which were then shuffled together and arranged in a stack. The Wonder Dog was next taught to go down through the stack, pawing at the ground to indicate which card was in each envelope, which it eventually did in the absence of Wood. The procedure was repeated several times, and the results showed that Chris scored significantly above chance. Chris therefore did possess a clairvoyant capability. This does not mean, however, that all dogs are as talented as Chris in this respect, for just as some dogs are more intelligent than others, so their extra-sensory abilities might be equally as varied, as in the case amongst ourselves.

Clairvoyance in cats has been investigated by two of Dr Rhine's co-workers, Dr K. Otis and Dr E. B. Foster, who presented an assortment of felines with food that was hidden from view under one of two cups, after having made sure that the cats could not be guided to the food by smell. If the animals had chosen a cup randomly, they would have selected the one with food underneath it about fifty per cent of the time. But they chose the right one at a rate well above the chance level, which showed that they had, like Chris, the Wonder Dog, clairvoyant skills.

The ability of both cats and dogs to psi-trail their owners is not only remarkable from a psychical point of view, but also says much for the will-power and persistence of the animals concerned. For in addition to making their way alone through a completely unfamiliar landscape, the deserted pets have also had to shift for themselves with regard to obtaining food, and have had to walk scores, sometimes hundreds, of miles. Yet such stories are often difficult to authenticate, especially in the case of cats, which are seldom provided with collars, as the animal that turns up at the door in a bedraggled condition may not in fact be the original animal, but simply one that looks like it and which is mistaken for it, something that can easily happen if several weeks have gone by since the move. And because the owner may not only be genuinely happy to have 'his' cat back again, but also get an ego-boost from its apparent battle through fire and flood and tempest to seek him out, his judgement may be suspended when it comes to positively identifying the animal.

And yet there are several well-authenticated accounts of cats that have psi-trailed their owners. Perhaps the best concerns the cat belonging to a New York veterinarian, which had a distinctive and very individual bony outgrowth on its fourth tail vertebra, which had resulted from it having been bitten by another cat. When the veterinarian moved to California, he gave the cat to a neighbour, never expecting to see it again. But see it again he did when, several months later, the animal strolled into his California home and immediately leaped onto its favourite chair. The vet was understandably amazed by its unexpected appearance, and quickly felt for the bony outgrowth to make sure that it really was his cat. The identification proved positive, showing that the cat had somehow made its way, alone and unaided, right across continental America, a distance of over two and a half thousand miles. A truly heroic journey!

An equally successful example of psi-trailing was demonstrated by Tony, a mongrel dog owned by a couple living at Aurora, Illinois, which was given to a neighbour when they moved 170 miles away to Lansing, Michigan, a town standing on the other side of Lake Michigan. They were likewise very surprised when, some six weeks later, Tony turned up at their door, panting and limping, wearing a tag on his collar that showed he had been temporarily adopted by another family en route. Tony had somehow skirted Lake Michigan and located his owners by ESP.

But it is not only mammals that have extra-sensory abilities. Research has shown that these are also possessed by fish, reptiles and birds, although such work has been limited, chiefly because of the difficulty of devising a suitable experimental method.

However, in 1967 Dr Morris published the results of a simple but ingenious experiment carried out with goldfish, which revealed that they could psychically tell when they were going to be picked out of the water in a net, something that fish do not particularly enjoy. Each fish that was to be netted was chosen by random selection and its behaviour compared to that of other fish just before the catch took place. Morris reported 'significant evidence of greater behavioural agitation' in the fish that was to be picked up, although this stress reaction lasted only a short time and was not continued if the delay between the intention to net it and the actual netting was long. This experiment did not show that fish had a precognitive insight into what was going to happen to them, but rather that they were warned of their fate by telepathy.

If such telepathic receptivity is generally possessed by fish it may account for the success of some fish in avoiding capture, like the proverbial pike that refuses to take the angler's worms. Hence the fish that are caught presumably have a less well-developed psychic sense than those that are not.

Perhaps more surprising is the discovery that certain non-mammalian animals have psychokinetic powers. Indeed, the paper titled 'Possible PK in the lizard *Anolis sagrei*', which was published in 1972 by G. K. Watkins and A. M. Watkins, suggests that not only do lizards possess psychokinetic ability but that this is more strongly developed in the females and in the dominant males. This positive result, with its sexual and personality variations, was gained by putting lizards in cages that were colder than they liked, but which they could warm up by triggering a switch by PK. And, as indicated, the subservient male lizards stayed cold.

Birds have long been regarded as having precognitive powers, and in ancient Rome the auspices (*auspicia* means 'bird watching') were regularly taken by observing the flight and listening to the song of certain birds. Legions on the march took chickens with them and divined the future from the way that they ate. When the sacred chickens refused to eat on being consulted by Claudius Pulcher during the First Punic War, he threw them into the Tiber, angrily shouting, 'Well, let them drink.' He should have heeded the feathered warning, however, for the expedition he subsequently mounted failed miserably.

My only experience of bird precognition happened some years ago when I interviewed Colin Kerr of Toronto, Canada, who had been travelling the country with Rajah, a prophetic mynah bird, which he touted as a 'legend of luck'. Rajah's method of spreading luck was deceptively simple – he did what all birds do naturally. His droppings were evidently as sacred as Aleister Crowley considered his to be, and Kerr told me, without the trace of a smile, that it was Rajah's ordure that had prevented any outbreak of violence at the 1976 Olympic Games.

Rajah's predictive powers were also formidable. According to Kerr the bird foretold President Nixon's resignation and the outcome of the next election. 'Carter wins' had emerged from Rajah's throat two days before the voting started. Improbable, yes, but facts are facts.

And of the future? Well, Rajah made two important predictions, one of which looks like coming true, while the other is less certain. The first was that the province of Quebec 'will never separate from Canada', and the second proclaimed that Colin Kerr will become the next biggest singing star of the world. Eleven years later the world is still waiting to hear one song by Colin Kerr.

Oh well, even a bird can't be right all the time!

Chapter 12
Astral Projection

In his book *Memories, Dreams, Reflections*, the psychiatrist Carl Jung recounts how, following a heart attack in 1944, he had a remarkable experience while unconscious. 'It seemed to me,' he writes, 'that I was high up in space. Far below me I saw the globe of the earth, bathed in a glorious blue light. I saw the deep blue sea and the continents. Far below my feet lay Ceylon, and in the distance ahead of me the subcontinent of India. My field of vision did not include the whole earth, but its global shape was plainly distinguishable and its outlines shone with a silvery gleam through that wonderful blue light . . . later I discovered how high in space one would have to be to have so extensive a view – approximately one thousand miles! The sight of the earth from this height was the most glorious thing I had ever seen.'

Although Jung called this occurrence a vision, it now seems that he had had an out-of-the-body experience or OBE. This happens when what we call our consciousness separates itself from the physical body, from where it can not only view that body from the outside but also travel, as did the consciousness of Carl Jung, to distant locations. And some people who have had OBEs have reported visiting non-physical realms that somehow co-exist with, but are separate from, our solid world of three dimensions.

Very interesting, you might say, but what has this to do with ESP? Quite simply, everything. If Jung did indeed see the earth from a great height, he was not observing it with his physical eyes but directly by means of his separated consciousness. Hence it was an extra-sensory perception, yet one differing from the often imprecise impressions that are gained by telepathy and clairvoyance in that it was sharp, clear and totally real. This suggests that the OBE may be the best and perhaps the only way of breaking completely through the 'mental noise' that throws a veil over our

Figure 16: The ancient Egyptians believed that the astral body had the form of a bird with a human face

psychic capabilities, to give us unrestricted views of distant places and perhaps of the past and future. It also strongly indicates that there might be a life after death.

In earlier literature, the out-of-the-body experience is called 'astral travelling' and the disassociated consciousness the 'astral body' or 'body of light'. The ancient Egyptians named the astral body the *ka*, which they pictured as having the form of a bird with a human face. At death, the ka flew away to the land of the dead, the consciousness separating itself permanently from the physical body that has been its home while the body was alive. The Greeks called it the *eidolon*, the ancient Britons the *fetch* or *task*. In fact almost every culture, both ancient and modern, has accounts of this inner part of ourselves, which is able to separate itself occasionally from the physical body during life and which certainly does so at death. And it is for this reason that we can identify it with the soul.

In normal circumstances the astral body only leaves the physical body when the latter is close to death, as happened with Dr Jung. There are many accounts of such separation by those who have had a heart attack or similar near-fatal health upset or accident – which is familiarly known as a near-death-experience or NDE – whereby they have suddenly found themselves outside their bodies, watching the scene in the hospital ward or at the site of the accident as if they were a third, and somewhat disinterested, party. Then, when the death of their body is prevented by the ensuing medical attention, they have been drawn back into it – to find themselves once more held fast in their physical cell. By no means all are happy to be returned to their body, as the following account illustrates. It was written by Sir Aukland (later Lord) Geddes, the professor of anatomy at Edinburgh University, who delivered it in an address to the Royal Medical Society of Edinburgh in 1937:

'On Saturday, 9 November . . . by ten o'clock, I had developed all the symptoms of very acute poisoning: intense gastro-intestinal pain, diarrhoea, pulse and respiration quite impossible to count. I wanted to ring for assistance, but found I could not, and so quite placidly gave up the attempt. I realized I was very ill . . . thereafter at no time did my consciousness appear to be in any way dimmed, but I suddenly realized that my consciousness was also separating from another consciousness which was also me. These, for purposes of description, we could call A and B consciousnesses, and throughout what follows (my awareness was attached) to the A consciousness . . . the A consciousness, which was now me, seemed to be altogether outside my body, which it could see. Gradually I realized that I could see, not only my body and the bed on which I was lying, but everything in the whole house and garden and then I realized that I was seeing, not only "things" at my home, but in London and Scotland . . . (Indeed) I had what appeared to be perfect two-eyed vision . . . Just as I was beginning to grasp all this, I saw "A" enter my bedroom. I realized that she got a terrible shock and I saw her hurry to the telephone. I saw my doctor leave his patients and come very quickly and I heard him say . . . "He is nearly gone" . . . I was really cross when he took a syringe and rapidly injected my body with something which I afterwards learned was camphor. As my heart began to beat more strongly, I was drawn back, and I was intensely annoyed, because I was so interested and was just beginning to understand where I was and what I was seeing. I came back into my body, really angry at being pulled back, and once back, all the clarity of vision of anything and everything disappeared, and I was just possessed of a glimmer of consciousness which was suffused with pain.'

But while such separations most often occur at moments of physical crisis, they also sometimes happen to those that are fit and well. In fact the results of several surveys reveal that spontaneous astral projection is comparatively common, with from ten per cent to forty-five per cent of those questioned claiming that it had happened to them. Yet because it is so strange in its nature, those who experience it tend to keep it quiet, fearing that they may be ridiculed or thought mad. It also usually happens only once in a person's life, when for some reason the conditions are right for it to take place. They were evidently right for a young Englishwoman in April 1970, when she was at home one afternoon in Canterbury:

'I had been lying on the sofa for a few hours, listening to my cousin playing the piano. I was completely relaxed and felt as if I was going to sleep. I felt a weight pressing down on my face and suddenly became aware that . . . I had actually risen to ceiling height. I turned over and seemed to hover . . . I could see everything in the room quite clearly, even myself lying on the sofa . . . Then I got what I can only describe as a coloured door floating in front of me. A voice within me seemed to say, "Open the door to seek knowledge." And as I moved toward it the door swung open to reveal a different coloured door. I remember thinking to myself that if I were to find an answer (but I didn't know to what) I had to travel on. I lost count of how many doors I went through but suddenly found myself way up in the sky hovering over Canterbury. Only it wasn't April any more; it was a summery day. But I had slight feelings of trepidation. What would happen if I travelled on into the unknown? As I was thinking about this I found myself staring down at my body again. I decided that I couldn't do it. Funny really – as soon as I had made my decision I was back in my body before you could say "Jack Flash".'

Such accounts necessarily imply that our consciousness is an independent entity that simply resides in the body, which is at odds with the prevailing scientific view that consciousness is nothing more than the brain's awareness of itself and the environment. Most scientists therefore think that astral projection is an impossibility and that consciousness ceases when the brain dies. Hence they would conclude that the experiences of Jung, Geddes and the young woman quoted above were vivid hallucinations, that is, subjective impressions and not an objective happening.

Yet there are two principal factors that go against this conclusion. The first derives from the nature of the OBE itself. Those to whom it has happened say that it was totally real and quite unlike a dream. Carl Jung himself said: 'I would never have imagined that any such experience was possible. It was not a product of imagination. The visions and experiences were utterly real; there was nothing subjective about them; they all had a quality of absolute objectivity.' The second stems from the fact that those who have had an OBE while unconscious are often able to later report on what was going on around them at the time, and sometimes of what was happening at a distant location. For example, a Frenchman who collapsed of heart failure in a London hotel in 1928 found that he separated from his body and floated to an upper corner of the room, from where he was able to watch the subsequent events:

'After an hour or two I heard a knock at the locked door several times, without being able to answer. Soon after, the hotel porter appeared on the fire escape. I saw him get into the room, look anxiously at my face, and open the door. The hotel manager and others entered. A physician came in. I saw him shake his head after listening to my heart, and then insert a spoon between my lips. I then lost consciousness and awoke in the bed.'

When he afterwards spoke with those concerned and described what he had seen, they were able to confirm his account of the events.

Similarly, in her book *Out-Of-The-Body Experiences*, Celia Green quotes a woman who had an OBE while in hospital, and who was able to later describe the condition of another patient who was ordinarily out of her view:

'One morning I felt myself floating upwards, and found I was looking down on the rest of the patients. I could see myself; propped up against pillows, very white and ill. I saw the sister and nurse rush to my bed with oxygen. Then everything went blank. The next thing I remember was opening my eyes to see the sister bending over me.

'I told her what had happened; but at first she thought I was rambling. Then I said, "There is a big woman sitting up in bed with her head wrapped in bandages; and she is knitting something with blue wool. She has a very red face." This certainly shook her; as apparently the lady concerned had had a mastoid operation and was just as I described.'

While some people who have an OBE say that they had no form as such, but were only a point of consciousness, others report that they had a shape. If so, the shape is sometimes a duplicate of their physical body, which means that they were aware of having arms, legs and so on, almost as though they had just 'stepped out' of themselves. It is this experience that has led to the astral body being called the 'double' or, to use the German term, *doppelgänger*, so-called because the person can on occasions be seen in this form. An American farmer named Walter McBride, who was worried at the time about the health of his father, had such an OBE in 1935. Separating from his body he passed effortlessly through the walls of his house and floated across the country to the home of his father, who lived several miles away.

'Going to the bedroom I stood at the foot of the bed in which I saw Father reclining. "Father," I said to him, "Father!" . . . he was watching me, for his eyes were fixed upon me and there seemed to be a look of surprise upon his face. The knowledge came to me as I stood there that he was well.

'A moment later I found myself leaving again . . . Reaching my bedroom once more I saw my own body, still lying on the bed where I had left it . . . Two days later, on Christmas Day, I paid Father a visit . . . Father verified my experience by stating that he had seen me, just as I had stood at the foot of the bed. He too had written down the time of his vision, and it tallied (with mine).'

But for others, while they also feel that they have a form, this is quite different from that of their physical body. Such was the case when, in 1983, a 72-year-old university don clinically died while undergoing treatment for cancer at London's Royal Marsden Hospital. Separating from his body he found himself in a strange landscape next to a tall dolmen.

'I am standing "in the shadow" (but there are no shadows here) of the great rock,' he wrote in the *Lancet*, recording the events as they happened. 'My shape is more or less that of a cube but is in the process of transformation, perhaps towards a globe. I am a living being, and my life is bliss and utter rightness, but a greater bliss and discovery are imminent. I rest in the power within and without me.

'This state of expectant aloneness is disturbed by the sudden appearance from behind the rock of a small group of beings. I can discern no bodies, but the faces are familiar. Their expressions are kind and compassionate. Alarm deepens to panic as they close in on me . . .'

The unwelcome newcomers turn out to be the professor's doctors, who, by employing their medical skill, restore him to life and in so doing drag his astral self away from the peace of that blissful landscape and back into his body. It was a resuscitation that he did not want to happen.

'For me, the experience was real,' he said afterwards. 'What happened was fact and an inevitable reality that I will soon face again. (But) I don't feel afraid to die any more. In fact, last night I started to think I should stop all these drugs and treatment and go home to my house in Crete . . . When I go next time I don't want them pulling me back.'

And again, there are reports of those, who, while disembodied, felt themselves to be 'oval in shape, about 2½ feet in breadth and about a foot in depth' and 'like a single eye that is lit up and about 2¼ inches in diameter'.

The astral body can pass with ease through solids like walls, and when moving it may float through the air or travel at great speed. It can also travel to a distant location instantly, this being brought about by the separated consciousness simply wishing to go there. And while some astral projectors, like Sylvan Muldoon, co-author of *The Phenomenon of Astral Projection*, have said that their astral body remains connected to the physical body by a cord-like thread, most claim that during separation they become completely free from their physical selves.

Over the years there have been a number of experiments carried out by parapsychologists who have attempted to ascertain if the OBE is an objective state or rather an hallucination accompanying the gathering of information by clairvoyant means. Such work has not proved easy, partly because of the difficulty of finding people who can consciously induce astral projection, and partly because of the difficulty of thinking up a suitable experimental method. This is perhaps why the results so far obtained have been ambiguous.

However, one quite clever experiment was devised by Dr Karlis Otis, the Director of Research at the American Society for Psychical Research, in 1975. He constructed a number of boxes, each of which contained a target picture, which when seen through the view-finder appeared in reverse, due to its being reflected by a mirror. He asked his subjects, who claimed to be able to astrally project, to separate from their bodies and look through each view-finder, and to report what they saw. In this way he hoped that if the targets were seen reversed, this would show that they had been viewed while out-of-the-body, whereas targets that were seen unreversed would presumably have been observed clairvoyantly. But unfortunately, while Dr Otis' results did indicate that the viewing was localized, they were only slightly above the chance expectation and therefore not by any means conclusive.

Scientists have also had little success in detecting the separated consciousness when they asked projectors to enter some sensitive field or device while in the disembodied state. The astral body has failed to register any instrumental response within infra-red or ultra-violet detectors, magnetometers and thermistors, although in one box containing an electrical field, Dr Otis found that 'the recorder went wild as if something had disturbed it' when one of his subjects projected into it.

Animals have proved more sensitive to the presence of the separated consciousness than machines. This much was demonstrated by an experiment carried out in 1978 by Dr Robert Morris at the Psychical Research Foundation in Durham, North Carolina. He caged four different types of animal, a gerbil, a hamster, a snake and a kitten, and carefully observed their normal behaviour. He then had Keith Harary, who claimed to be able to induce himself to astrally project, to send his separated consciousness into each of the four cages. Morris recorded what effect, if any, this had on the animals. The two rodents showed no change in behaviour, but the snake became noticeably upset. 'It started literally to attack,' wrote co-researcher Scott Rogo. 'It sort of bit the air viciously, for about twenty seconds – twenty seconds which were right in the middle of the time that Keith, without knowing what was going on in the laboratory, claimed to be out of his body and in the cage with the snake.' The cat also reacted, although quite differently. When Harary projected into its cage, it quietened down considerably. 'It stopped running around the cage, did not miaow once,' noted Morris, 'and seemed to be attentive to a presence in the enclosure that no human in the room could perceive.'

Morris repeated the experiment four more times and observed the same behavioural changes in the snake and the kitten. So something was going on, but what exactly? Had Keith Harary actually projected into the cages housing the animals or had he affected their behaviour by telepathic control or perhaps by psychokinesis? The conclusion, at least as far as the reality of the OBE is concerned, was equivocal.

But we have met with several people who have experienced a spontaneous astral separation, and also the odd individual like Keith Harary who claims to be able to induce the experience at will. The latter has perhaps had you wondering if you could do the same. How, then, does one astrally project?

The short answer to that is, with great difficulty. Of those who have had OBEs, only a very few have been able to make it happen. This indicates that our consciousness is tightly bound to our physical self, and that its dislodgement is extremely hard to bring about. I know this for a fact. Over the years I have tried on many occasions to astrally project, but have so far only managed to completely separate my conscious self from my physical self once. I will tell you how I did it and describe the different stages of the process, and what it is like to be free from the prison of the body. But having said that, I can offer no guarantee that the technique I used will work for you – indeed, it hasn't since worked again, yet, for me.

The physical props you will need are a comfortable bed or couch, upon which you will lie, and quiet surroundings. Traffic and aeroplane noise, or that made by the family or neighbours, will effectively prevent astral separation.

The time of day that one makes the attempt is important. It is best done in the evening with the lights off and the room dark. This is so for two reasons. First, the darkness of the room creates a corresponding darkness in one's head, whereas if one lies in a sunlit or an electrically lit room, the light filtering through the eyelids makes the mental state I later describe more difficult to attain. Second, the light tiredness one feels in the evening is conducive to astral separation, making it easier to quieten the mind. Daytime attempts are impeded by the greater amount of brain activity, while those made very late at night usually end in one going to sleep.

Lie on your back, either on or in the bed, with your head raised somewhat by one or two pillows. Wear your pyjamas or nightdress, or some equally comfortable attire. Make sure you are warm enough. Cold feet distract the mind and hinder separation. So also do physical aches and pains. Your nasal passages should allow a free flow of air when you breathe. A partially blocked nose will create an irritating noise, which again is distracting. The quieter and less obtrusive you can make your breathing, the better. You must also remain undisturbed. Thus, if necessary, take the telephone off the hook and instruct anyone else in the house to be quiet and to leave you alone.

When I first started trying to astrally project I attempted to force my consciousness to leave my body, even going so far as to repeat a phrase like 'out of my body, out of my body' over and over again. That proved useless. You cannot will yourself as such to leave your body. I also followed the advice given by those who claimed that they had achieved separation, by picturing myself hovering above my physical body and then willing my consciousness to move into this mental construct. That likewise proved negative. In fact, such methods did not even precipitate the interior events that eventually led to my astral separation.

I was therefore obliged to seek alternatives and by a process of trial and error I managed to find the key to the experience, although I must add that the key was very hard to turn. This is because the absolutely quiet inner state that allows separation is difficult to obtain and sustain. But without it, if my experience is anything to go by, astral projection cannot occur.

This quiet inner state is brought about by stopping one's normal thought processes, by in other words emptying the mind. One's consciousness thereby becomes a silent, dark void, from which everyday thoughts and concerns are completely excluded. This naturally also means that you must not even think about astral projection. Of course, you lie down intending to astrally project, but having once formulated the intention you forget about it. The act of separation will happen automatically if you follow the steps I have outlined. But a lot of practice will be necessary before you can get your thoughts under control, so be patient.

This state of mental quietness is the goal of meditation, which mystics throughout the ages have said is the one way to Nirvana, or enlightenment, whereby the mind, having divorced itself from the world of sense impressions, allows itself to make contact with not only the non-material world but ultimately with God or the divine. This is why Dionysus the Areopagite wrote: 'Into this supreme and dazzling darkness we pray that we may come, that by not seeing and not knowing we may see and know him who is beyond all seeing and knowing through this very act of not seeing or knowing; and at this supreme peak of being, by dismissing all things that *are*, that we may praise him who is himself above all.'

As you get your mind under control, you will almost certainly experience a number of interesting physical and mental phenomena, which in themselves indicate that you are heading in the right direction. You may feel, for instance, a soft breeze blowing across your face and hear a high-pitched, but by no means unpleasant, whine in your ears. And inwardly you may see a variety of forms take shape that arise on their own and therefore have nothing to do with your own thought processes, these of course having been stilled. I remember that when I first used this technique, I often saw a procession of faces appear in my consciousness, which came, as it were, to silently look at me, as if wondering what I was doing. The faces belonged to both men and women, and were of all ages, young, middle-aged and old. I do not know if they rose up from my own subconscious or if they were the denizens of some spiritual world. But whatever their origins, they were quite harmless and eventually ceased appearing. You may also see a variety of coloured patterns and spots of light, which move and interweave with each other, sometimes taking on a stunning complexity. By all means enjoy these sights, yet do not allow them to reactivate your thoughts. They are merely signposts along the way, and should be treated as such. However, it is interesting to note that these coloured patterns are very similar to those produced by the ingestion of a hallucinogenic drug like LSD or mescaline. In his book *Drugs*, Peter Laurie points out that while as little as twenty microgrammes of LSD can produce a detectable effect, the even smaller amount that gets to the brain 'has left (it) within twenty minutes of taking the drug, while the effects of the dose do not begin in less than thirty minutes to one hour, and last for four to eight hours. It is supposed, therefore, that the hallucinogens act as triggers, releasing some body chemical that produces the celebrated psychic effects.' This implies that meditation releases the same chemical.

If you manage to sustain this image-producing state, you will find that in due course your consciousness will seemingly grow larger, as if the volume of your head had somehow increased. If so, this will happen quite suddenly and with an almost audible click. It will be accompanied, if this has not happened before, by a whining or a buzzing, and perhaps by a movement, as it were, of your consciousness, such as a gentle swaying from side to side. This is a most important stage in the process of astral projection because it represents a loosening of your consciousness from its connections within the brain. It is a point, therefore, of incipient astral projection.

Yet having reached it, this does not mean that full separation will automatically occur. This is usually because it generates certain anxieties about what might happen if one goes further. After all, you are treading very much into the unknown and it is natural to feel afraid of where you might end up. We have all heard tales about demons and hobgoblins and evil spirits, and it may seem that by astrally projecting we could somehow deliver ourselves into their power. But such fears are irrational and must be conquered. I had them myself, yet I persevered. And for what it's worth, I have never come across any sign of threatening beings, which I now believe belong to the world of the imagination, not to the world of reality.

Once the bonds of consciousness have been released, the next step is for the remainder of the astral self, which occupies the body, to do the same. This results in a shaking and shuddering within one's whole self, and this also happens quite suddenly and unexpectedly. It is a stage in the process that is very difficult to describe, for it is not a movement of one's physical self, but of the astral component of that self. Hence it is unlike any shaking and shuddering that you might have otherwise experienced, as when you perhaps were ill and suffering from a fever.

But although this odd movement immediately precedes astral projection, I must again say that astral projection does not always follow it. I have many times attained this state, but for reasons that are still mysterious to me, have not been able to go further. But it is the last step in the sequence and it can lead to the grand sweep of astral projection, which I will now describe.

My own experience of full separation took place one night in Montreal in the autumn of 1976, when I stayed with my girlfriend. It may be relevant to record that I had drunk two bottles of brown ale and smoked several cigarettes before retiring. Then, after my girlfriend and I had made love, while she went to sleep I got down to the serious business of astrally projecting, a task that was made less daunting by her presence. The room was dark and quiet, and I was suitably tired and relaxed. I was quite determined, however, that I would not fall asleep.

I began, as I have outlined above, by clearing my mind and stilling my thoughts. This eventually brought me to the 'consciousness expanding' stage, from which, disappointingly, I gradually withdrew. I tried again, with the same result. Indeed, I had to get to that point a further two or three times before the 'shaking and shuddering' ensued. I have no idea how long that took, but it was perhaps about two or three hours.

When the shaking and shuddering had gone on for a little while, I heard a noise like a rushing wind, which suddenly erupted to accompany it. Then, quite contrary to my expectations, I was swept towards my feet, pulled as if by some invisible hand through a dark void, the rushing noise increasing in volume as I moved. I say 'quite contrary to my expectations' because in all the accounts of consciously-willed astral projection that I had read, the astral body of the person concerned moved either upwards or, as in some instances, downwards; hence I had anticipated a similar direction of movement. I emerged from the darkness, the sound ceasing as I did so, to find myself apparently kneeling on all fours at the end of the bed, facing toward the windows on the opposite side of the room. But I did not know at that moment that I had left my physical self behind, because I felt as if the whole of me was kneeling there. I was aware of having arms and legs, although I did not look at them. The portion of the room that I could see looked exactly as it did when I viewed it through my physical eyes: it was not imbued with an etheric light or anything like that. I remember turning and looking off to my right, and what I saw was palpably real. Indeed, had it not been for what happened next I would not have believed that my consciousness had separated from my physical self.

What took place next was odd, because as I looked further to my right my girlfriend suddenly appeared beside me, kneeling like I was on the end of the bed, looking perfectly solid and lifelike. She did not say anything, but as our eyes met I was instantly returned to my physical body, waking up with a jolt within it, to find myself still lying on my back with the bedclothes pulled up to my chin. And it was only then that I knew I had been out of my body, for the experience while out of it had been so real. I sat up, amazed by what had happened and full of wonder. It was only later that I wished I had been more on the ball and had taken the opportunity to explore my disembodied state more fully.

In the morning I told my girlfriend what had happened and asked her if she recalled kneeling beside me. But alas, she remembered no such thing; her sleep had been peaceful and apparently uneventful. I should of course have woken her immediately. I might then have received a different response.

I can only presume that my separation had somehow drawn her astral self from her body while she slept. For what happened to me was not a dream; its quality was quite different. It had been, as was Jung's experience, utterly real.

I have given this account of my own OBE to perhaps prepare you for something similar should you wish to attempt such separation yourself. I can only again warn you that it is extremely difficult to bring about, and you must expect a long, hard battle before you achieve it. I am still trying, when conditions permit, to repeat my first experience and perhaps when it happens I will be able to take another step into the unknown.

Chapter 13
Life After Death

'I'm tired, tired of being enclosed here. I'm wearying to escape into that glorious world, and to be always there: not seeing it dimly through tears, and yearning for it through the walls of an aching heart; but really with it, and in it.'

Catherine in *Wuthering Heights.*

If the consciousness can separate from the physical body, as the accounts of such separation mentioned in the last chapter indicate, this means that we may survive the death of our bodies. It is relevant to not only examine this possibility more fully, but to see what light it sheds, if any, on the fact of ESP.

The belief in a life after death is as old as man. Every age and culture has entertained it, which in the past often led to the deceased being provided with food, clothing and tools to help them survive and function in the next world. Yet such concern for the welfare of the dead was surely mistaken, because the separated consciousness or soul is non-physical and has no need of the things that sustain physical life.

But while the belief in a life after death is ancient, it is only comparatively recently that it has become possible to investigate this belief scientifically. This has been due largely to the advance of medical knowledge, which has allowed the resuscitation of those who have clinically died. For it is their accounts of what they experienced while dead, which were first brought to public awareness by Dr Raymond Moody in his book *Life After Life*, published in 1975, that has in part shown that the ancient beliefs are more than a pious hope.

Dr Moody interviewed over one hundred people who had clinically died and who had reported having undergone certain strange experiences while dead. From these he was able to piece together a model of the principal stages of the experience and the order in which they generally took place. None of the people interviewed had had them all, but all had experienced one or more of them.

Typically, Dr Moody found that at the time the hospitalized patient's heart stops beating, he (or she) hears the doctor pronounce him dead. He then becomes aware of a noise like a ringing or a buzzing, which is usually described as 'unpleasant', while at the same time feeling himself drawn out of his body through a darkness, as if he were travelling down a tunnel. He next finds himself outside his body, floating in the air, from where he is able to watch the activity that is taking place in the ward or, if the medical crisis has taken place outdoors, at the scene of the accident.

But although this separation happens suddenly and unexpectedly, the person quickly adjusts to it and begins to enjoy it. Indeed, he feels no regret at having died. He is aware that he has a form, although one quite different from his physical self. He may also, at this time, meet with the spirits of relatives and friends who have already died, who assure him, if need be, that all is well.

He then has an encounter with a very special spiritual entity, which appears as a radiantly bright, whiteish light. This 'being of light' is totally warm, loving and welcoming, and the dead person feels great peace and contentment in its presence. The light asks him non-verbal questions to enable him to evaluate his life. He is helped in this by being shown a rapid and colourful panoramic 'playback of the major events of his life'. He may also be asked if he feels he is ready to die.

The being of light then leads him to a barrier, which may be seen as a line or a wall, or as some other divide, that marks the end-point of earthly existence. He understands that if he crosses it, he cannot return to this life. Yet although he wants to cross it, he realizes that because he still has certain responsibilities or unfulfilled tasks that require his attention in the physical world, he must return to his body. This immediately happens, and he wakes up in his physical body, having at that moment been resuscitated by the doctors and nurses attending him.

The preliminary stages of this remarkable experience are very similar to those reported by people who have had an OBE. This suggests that it is the same bodily element, the consciousness, that leaves the body at death. However, Dr Moody's findings, indicating as they do that there is an existence beyond death, have been criticized by those who believe that the events described by the dying can be explained in other ways. It has been suggested, for instance, that they may be caused by the drugs administered at the time or by the malfunctioning of the brain as it is deprived of oxygen, which would make them subjective and not objective, hallucinations and not reality. But such objections are countered by not only the subjects' sense that what was happening to them was real, but by the fact that neither the drugs employed nor a lack of brain oxygen create the same phenomena in those whose lives are not at risk.

But perhaps more damaging is the objection that the events happened to people who had not really died, whose physical condition was such that it allowed their resuscitation. This is of course true, but so also is the fact that the people concerned knew that they had a choice as to whether they returned to their bodies or not, that they felt they were still on the 'life' side of the dividing barrier, and that they made the decision to return. Had they decided otherwise, they would presumably have been incapable of resuscitation.

Fascinating though this topic is, it does fall somewhat outside the scope of this book and so I shall not discuss the overall nature of the after-death experience further. But I do recommend those who are interested in finding out more to read *Life After Life*, and Dr Moody's other book, *Reflections on Life After Life*, as well as the similar works by writers like Dr Elisabeth Kübler-Ross.

There are, however, certain elements of the after-death experience that are relevant to our examination of extra-sensory perception. These are the perceptual experiences of the disembodied person.

Many of Dr Moody's interviewees said that when they separated from their bodies they no longer possessed a sense of taste or smell, yet at the same time their visual and auditory perceptions became much more acute. One man said, 'I just can't understand how I could see so far.' And a woman reported, 'It seemed as if this spiritual sense had no limitations, as if I could look anywhere and everywhere.'

But while things could be seen and sounds heard with greater clarity, these perceptions were extra-sensory. This was graphically indicated by the experience of another woman, who said, 'When I wanted to see someone at a distance, it seemed like a part of me, kind of like a tracer, would go to that person.' And where hearing is concerned, Dr Moody remarks that '*Hearing* in the spiritual state can apparently be called so only by analogy, and most say that they do not really hear physical voices and sounds. Rather, they seem to pick up the thoughts of the persons around them.' And he illustrated this by quoting a woman who said, 'I could see people all around, and I could understand what they were saying. I didn't hear them, audibly, like I'm hearing you. It was more like knowing what they were thinking, exactly what they were thinking, but only in my mind, not in their actual vocabulary. I would catch it the second before they opened their mouths to speak.'

This direct transfer of thoughts, which we would call telepathy, also takes place when the separated consciousness encounters the being of light. 'People claim,' says Moody, 'that they did not hear any physical voice or sounds from the being, nor did they respond to the being through audible sounds. Rather, it is reported that direct, unimpeded transfer of thoughts takes place, and in such a clear way that there is no possibility whatsoever of either misunderstanding or lying to the light. Furthermore, this unimpeded exchange does not even take place in the native language of the person. Yet, he understands perfectly and is instantaneously aware.'

From this we can conclude that not only are the perceptions of the separated consciousness both perfectly clairvoyant and telepathic, but are also, with the help of the being of light, retrocognitive as well. Thus communication while out of the body is by ESP, whose effectiveness is greatly enhanced by the disembodied state. This implies that we all have latent ESP faculties, which are somehow prevented from fully manifesting by the body in which we reside. In this sense we are like prisoners in solitary confinement who can only communicate with one another by tapping on the pipes of their cells. Some interaction is possible, yet this is greatly inferior to what could be achieved if they were allowed to meet and talk with one another.

The discovery by some of Moody's interviewees that there is a border between this life and the next is of particular interest as it corresponds to the wall that many ancient peoples believed surrounded the land of the dead, entry to which was gained by the passage through one or more gates. We also find this in popular Christianity, wherein the Pearly Gates give access to heaven or paradise.

But not all the ancients thought that the underworld was surrounded by a wall. The Greeks, for example, said that Tartarus, Hades' realm, was separated from the upper world by a river, the Styx, over which the souls of the dead were ferried by Charon, whose name, interestingly enough, means 'fierce brightness'. Likewise, the Vikings said that the souls of ordinary mortals had to cross a wide sea to reach the hall of Geirrod the giant:

'It was needful to sail over the ocean that goes around the lands, to leave the sun and the stars behind, to journey down into chaos, and at last to pass into a land where no light was and where darkness reigned eternally.'

Dr Moody talked with two people who had experienced a journey across water to reach the beyond. One revealed: 'When you get on the other side, there's a river . . . it had a smooth surface, just like glass . . . Yeah, you cross a river. I did.' The other sailed across a stretch of water on a boat. 'The next thing I knew it seemed to me as if I was on a ship or a small vessel sailing to the other side of a large body of water. On the distant shore, I could see all of my loved ones who had died – my mother, my father, my sister, and others . . . Finally, the ship almost reached the far shore, but just before it did, it turned around and started back . . . it was at this point, I guess, that I came around, and the doctor explained what had happened, that I had had a post-partum haemorrhage, and that they had nearly lost me.'

It may well be that the ancients derived their beliefs from the testimony of those few of their fellows who had been revived from clinical death, whose return would have seemed miraculous. The Venerable Bede (AD 673–735) tells of one man 'who led a devout life with all his household. He fell ill and grew steadily worse until the crisis came, and in the early hours of the night he died. But at daybreak he returned to life and suddenly sat up to the great consternation of those weeping around the body, who ran away.' He told his wife, the only one who did not flee from his bedside, what had happened to him while he was dead. 'A handsome man in a shining robe was my guide . . . he soon brought me out of the darkness into an atmosphere of clear light, and as he led me forward in a bright light, I saw before us a tremendous wall which seemed to be of infinite length and height in all directions. As I could see no gate, window, or entrance in it, I began to wonder why we went up to the wall. But when we reached it, all at once – I know not by what means – we were on top of it. Within lay a very broad and pleasant meadow . . . Such was the light flooding all this place that it seemed greater than the brightness of daylight or of the sun's rays at noon . . .'

Lastly, it seems entirely reasonable to suppose that if our consciousness is a separate entity that simply resides in our body while it is alive, and which departs from it at death, then it may, after a suitable sojourn in the realm of the dead, be reborn into another body at a later date. This concept, which is called reincarnation, although closely associated with Buddhist and other Eastern beliefs, was originally widely accepted throughout the Christian world until it was condemned as a heresy by the Emperor Justinian in the sixth century AD. Indeed, Origen, an early Christian writer, said: 'Every soul comes into this world strengthened by the victories or weakened by the defeats of its previous life.'

Thus it may be that our bodies are temporary refuges of our souls. If so, we have probably lived before, and will no doubt do so again.

Chapter 14
Further Communication

'You know, I was wild after she died; and eternally, from dawn to dawn, praying for her to return to me – her spirit – I have a strong faith in ghosts: I have a conviction that they can, and do exist, among us.'

Heathcliff in *Wuthering Heights*

When the consciousness leaves the body at death to make its way to another realm, with its awareness sharpened by unobstructed ESP, could it at some stage make contact with those who are left behind? Might communication with the dead therefore be possible?

Members of the spiritualist churches have no doubt that such communication can and does take place. They say that the souls of the departed continue to take an interest in what is happening 'down here' and will, when asked, give both comfort and advice to the living. The dead have also described what their existence is like beyond the grave.

Yet spirits do, however, have trouble in communicating directly with most people, which is why they generally talk through specially trained human intermediaries called mediums. 'A medium,' states a definition adopted by the National Spiritualist Association of Churches, 'is one whose organism is sensitive to vibrations from the spirit world and through whose instrumentality intelligences in that world are able to convey messages and produce the phenomena of Spiritualism.'

Some years ago, while researching an article on spiritualism for the *Montreal Gazette* newspaper, I attended services at each of the five spiritualist churches in Montreal and spoke at length to a number of the mediums. The latter told me that quite a lot is known about the life hereafter.

'After death,' said Michael (mediums are usually known only by their first names), 'you firstly go to a resting place if you have died of something like cancer. You need rest because the spirit body has been left weak from the illness. When your strength is regained you're taken to a sphere where you'll get your rightful reward.'

Another, William, a medium at the rather grandly named International Temple of Spiritual Revelations, said that when someone 'passes over' he or she is met by relatives and friends already on the 'other side'.

'You are allowed to spend some time with them,' he explained. 'Then you'll be visited by a high spiritual master and be taken away to the Hall of Memories. There you'll come before your self. You see all your past life, all your rights and wrongs, and you will judge yourself. God does not judge you. You must compensate for all the wrongs you have done. Everyone has some debt to pay.

'Afterwards you begin to progress through the higher spheres. Your goal is to attain the kingdom of God. During your progress through the spheres you will be called upon to help others as a guide – but this helps you to progress to the higher spheres.'

Each of us, according to the spiritualists, has one or more spirit guides. And while most of us are quite unaware of their presence, those who train to become mediums learn how to both sense and communicate with them.

'I'm familiar with five or six of my guides,' said Elizabeth. 'My "doorkeeper" is Running Water, an Indian. Different guides are used for different phases of our work. One will come forward for healing, another for something else. Running Water selects who I'm going to use and so acts as a screen. You know who the guides are because you sense different vibrations from them.'

And Esther told me: 'I have a master guide named Master David. He's at the head. I also have an Indian guide called White Cloud. My doctor guide is Dr Thomas Dooley and my chemist guide is Dr George Washington Carver. I also have a joy guide named Annabel. She brings joy to people and contacts spirits in the trumpet circle.'

The trumpet circle is a special séance wherein the medium goes into a trance and through whom the spirits speak in the same voices they had while alive. At the one I attended, which was held in a completely dark room, trumpets like hunting horns that had been coated with luminous paint were apparently levitated by spirit hands. It was not, however, a convincing demonstration.

Mediums are trained by the spiritualist churches at their development classes. While some people are natural mediums and require little training, others may have to study for many months before they acquire their 'gift' or 'gifts'.

Elizabeth, for example, has developed three gifts. She does message work, which means that she can contact the dead, heal and give 'discourses' or lectures. The latter gift also involves contact with a spirit, who speaks through the medium. Elizabeth told me what it is like being taken over by a spirit prior to delivering a discourse.

'It's like a veil coming over you, as though you've released your brain for a spirit,' she said. 'You just stand aside and let somebody else use your vocal cords. I also feel very cold. I'm particularly aware of my hands being cold.'

The discourses are usually about the nature of life in the spirit world and the meaning of human existence. They are invariably uplifting in tone. For instance, one medium said in her discourse:

'You are spirit before you are anything else. You choose your parents; they do not choose you. Having children is soul mating and the decision to give another soul earth experience. You are each on the earth plane for a purpose . . .

'How sad it is to think that death is the end of everything. Death instead is a stepping stone into another world of God's love. We don't stop at death – we progress. Death is a joy.'

Services at a spiritualist church are broadly similar to those of a 'low' Protestant church. Hymns are sung and one or two prayers are said. But little time is actually spent on worship. Instead the service centres around a lengthy discourse and the messages from the departed which are given to the congregation by one of the mediums.

Billet reading is sometimes employed by the mediums. For this the members of the congregation each write down the names of two or three deceased persons and a question they would like answered on a piece of paper. The papers are then folded and given to the medium, who, holding each in turn, will try to get 'something through' from the spirit world.

'The guides do the work,' explained Solly. 'We're just the instrument. With billet reading it's not a case of being accurate, it's what one gets from spirit. The ones upstairs give it to us and we tell the person. Often they don't recognize anything we say.'

But while I did not doubt the sincerity of these mediums, it did strike me that many of the messages that they purportedly received from the spirits were very general in nature and often cloyingly optimistic. Everything will 'improve' or 'get better' for the subject of the message, who is urged to 'look outwards' or promised that 'you'll shortly see a light at the end of the tunnel'. Helpful sentiments, I agree, but hardly suggestive that the messages are really coming from the spirit world. And where factual information is concerned, it seemed that the medium's telepathic and clairvoyant abilities operating in this world were sufficient to account for the information received, rather than concluding that they extended to the next.

This is not to say that all supposed contacts by the dead result from the medium mistaking the source of her information. The Society for Psychical Research has many thousands of spirit contact cases on record that cannot be explained away by telepathy, clairvoyance, retrocognition or even fraud. These suggest that not only is there an existence beyond the grave, but that communication with the dead is possible.

And yet communication with disembodied spirits does not, indeed cannot, take place for the average person in the same way that it perhaps does with the medium. For even if the separated consciousness has excellent powers of ESP, as some of Moody's subjects indicated, which enable it to read the thoughts of the living, this does not mean that it can communicate its thoughts any better with those who are still alive. In fact many of those who clinically died tried desperately to stop the medical personnel from resuscitating them. 'Please, please, let me alone,' begged the professor mentioned in the last chapter. 'You are destroying me. Oh, why do you do this to me? I have never injured you . . . Stop, for pity's sake!' But despite these pleas the resuscitation attempt proceeds, and the man is revived. 'I apologize to my doctors for the same continuance of dread into "waking" life,' he added. 'Did they, I wonder, see or feel anything of it?' The answer is, no, they didn't. His attempt at communicating with them had been futile.

The separated consciousness also lacks physical substance, and this means that it is unable to impress itself upon solid objects to the extent of moving them. There are many accounts written by those who have tried, while undergoing an OBE, to affect their surroundings in some way, with disappointing results. After all, if the separated consciousness can pass though walls, ceilings and even blocks of granite without hindrance, it is perhaps not surprising that it has difficulty in knocking a favourite vase off the mantlepiece. But more importantly, it also means that while the separated consciousness may have heightened ESP, it lacks any psychokinetic ability. It cannot, in other words, move objects by willing them to do so.

Yet the separated consciousness can, at least on occasions, make its presence known visually. We have seen how the person undergoing an OBE sometimes appears as a *doppelgänger* or double, while the dead person may materialize as a ghost. However, both *doppelgängers* and ghosts are rarely seen, which suggests that the ability of the separated consciousness to manifest in this way is limited. Indeed, all those persons who had clinically died and found themselves out of their bodies told Dr Moody that they were quite invisible to the doctors, nurses and other people who were present.

But as we have seen, our ESP is heightened in certain mental states, as when our minds are quiet and relaxed, when we are asleep and when we are in a trance. These are the conditions in which we are more receptive, not only to the thoughts of the living, but also to the presence of the dead. This explains why the best mediums have to go into a trance before they can receive messages from the 'other side'. It likewise explains why we often get a sense of contact with departed loved ones and friends in our dreams. And sometimes the dead may impart information to the dreamer that is of benefit to him.

For example, consider the case of Dr Hilprecht, a professor of Assyrian at Pennsylvania University, who had a dream that enabled him to solve an archaeological puzzle. This took place in 1883, when the academic was having difficulty in deciphering the cuneiform characters on two small pieces of agate, which he had found in the temple of Bel or Marduk at Nippur. Hilprecht believed that they had been part of two rings, but because of their size and the few characters that each bore, he was dubious about being able to read what the characters said. All he had by way of a clue were the letters KU, and from this he thought that the original rings might have belonged to the Kassite king Kurigalzu II (c. 1345–1324 BC).

Then one night, after having worked late, he went to bed and dreamed that he was in the temple of Bel. He was approached by a tall, middle-aged priest wearing a long white robe. The priest led him to a windowless treasure chamber on the south side of the temple, which contained a large treasure chest and on whose floor lay several pieces of agate and lapis lazuli.

The priest told the professor that the two fragments of agate he had were not parts of rings, but came from earrings that had been made for the statue of the god Ninib or Ninurta, the 'champion of the celestial gods', whose warlike nature had once caused the whole of nature to rise up against him, with the exception of certain stones that allied themselves to him. On Ninib's victory, he blessed those stones and gave them a special brilliance, turning them into gems like agate, lapis lazuli and amethyst. Each earring had been made from a part of the votive cylinder that King Kurigalzu II had sent to the temple. This was done because, when the priests received orders to make the earrings for the god's statue out of agate, the only agate available was that of the votive cylinder.

'The cylinder was cut into three parts,' explained the priest. 'Two parts were made into earrings for the god, and the third part was lost. Put the two pieces of agate that you have together and you will find that they match up. This will enable you to read the inscription on them.' The priest then disappeared, and the dream ended.

The following day Professor Hilprecht decided to do what the dream priest had said. He hurried to the university, took up the two pieces of agate and held them together. This completed certain of the cuneiform characters and allowed the professor to decipher what they said, which was: 'To the god Ninib, son of Bel his lord, has Kurigalzu, pontifex of Bel, presented this.' The dream priest had been right!

And here is another instance of how a separated consciousness, appearing in a dream, proved useful to the dreamer. This is of particular interest, not only because the dream resulted in a child's life being saved, but because the separated consciousness originated from a dog.

In 1980 Lady, the much-loved Labrador dog of Walter Manuel, a resident of Los Angeles, died. During the three weeks following Lady's death, the distressed owner dreamed of her four times. Each dream was pleasant in itself, yet unusual in that water formed a common thread that linked them. In the first dream Manuel saw Lady swimming across a lake to retrieve a duck he had shot; in the second Lady was gambolling in the surf while the family was on holiday; in the third the dog was with him as he did some angling in a trout stream; and in the fourth Lady jumped into the swimming pool in the garden to collect a stick that he had thrown for her.

Walter Manuel could understand why he dreamed about his beloved Lady, but was puzzled by the ever-present water. 'I wonder why this is?' he said to his wife. 'There were so many other things that we did together.'

Four nights after the last dream, Manuel again dreamed about the dog, except that instead of seeing her, he only heard her frantically barking, just as she had done when some prowlers had entered the garden. On that occasion Manuel had jumped out of bed, grabbed his rifle and gone quickly to the window to frighten them off.

The dream also had him rushing to the window, where he was stunned to see his two-year-old son Jason kneeling on the edge of the swimming pool, reaching out to the bright reflection of the full moon in the water. As the child fell in, he raced down to the pool and was in time to rescue him from drowning. The dream had enabled him to save his son.

'Nothing will shake my conviction,' he said afterwards, 'that in some way that cannot be explained, Lady actually warned me of the danger. It is just what she would have done if she had been alive.'

If Lady did warn her master, from beyond the pale of death, that his son was in danger of drowning, it naturally suggests that dogs undergo the same sort of consciousness separation as we do when they die. And if this happens to dogs, then why shouldn't it also happen to cats, horses, rabbits, rats and mice, and indeed to every other sort of animal, as well as possibly plants? After all, why should we be the only creatures that have souls? Other living things are so similar to us physiologically, that it would be quite extraordinary if they were unlike us in this respect. And anyway, there have been sufficient sightings of spectral dogs, cats and horses to suggest that at least these animals survive death.

Yet neither of the two examples mentioned above necessarily prove that the dreamer was actually contacted by a separated consciousness. Professor Hilprecht might have noticed, without being consciously aware of it, that the two pieces of agate could be fitted together, which would mean that his dream was simply his brain's way of bringing this observation to his attention. It is also hard to understand why the separated consciousness of a priest who had been dead for three thousand years would want to help him resolve such an unimportant mystery.

And Walter Manuel's own psychic faculties could explain his dreams. Precognition would account for the first four dreams, in which Lady was seen in water, especially if, on the night when he had seen his son at the edge of the swimming pool, he had coincidently heard a live dog barking; while his arousal from sleep on that night might have been brought about by him clairvoyantly sensing that his son was in danger, or he might have been entirely fortunate in being woken by a neighbour's dog – although this would not explain why it stopped barking the moment he woke up.

But if the dead can contact us while we sleep, they also have other methods at their disposal. I know this from personal experience. Let me give you one example.

In 1972 I interviewed an elderly Englishman who ran a small art boutique in old Montreal, where he sold sketches, water-colour paintings and wood sculptures that he had crafted himself. What was unusual about him was that, as a convinced spiritualist, he claimed his hands were guided by the dead, who thus worked through him.

At the end of the interview he told me that he was also a psychometrist and that he would, if I agreed, see what he could get from some object of mine. I gave him first my watch and then the medallion I wore around my neck. He had no success with these; nothing, he said, was coming through.

I was disappointed and a little piqued. Did this mean, I wondered, that he was a bit of a fraud?

But then he did something that was quite extraordinary.

'There's a spirit here,' he suddenly announced. 'He's a relative of yours. His name is Walter.'

I sat up. For yes, I did have a deceased relative named Walter. From what I remembered he had been one of my father's uncles.

'I'm going to put my hands over my face,' he went on, 'and when I take them away Walter's face will appear on mine.'

As I watched, somewhat startled, he brought his hands up to his face, held them there for a few seconds and then lowered them. His face had undergone an amazing transformation, for without in any way him contorting his features, it had become another face. The skin had become tighter, the forehead more domed, the cheeks thinner, and the eyes hollower. It was immediately obvious to me that it belonged to a member of my mother's family, whose name was Cole, and not to my father's. It was quite definitely a Cole face.

I had witnessed something that spiritualists call transfiguration, and I was suitably impressed. I was even more impressed when I later discovered that Walter was a brother of my maternal grandfather, which made him a Cole. He had died in 1960.

The English artist could not have picked up anything from me about Walter telepathically. For not only had I never met Walter, but had mistakenly thought that he belonged to the other side of the family.

I have no idea why great-uncle Walter should have wanted to put on such a spectacular appearance for me, unless of course he hoped that by doing so he would demonstrate that the dead are not dead, but simply someplace else.

If so, I was totally convinced.

Epilogue

I hope that the accounts I have given of the scientific experiments into extra-sensory perception, and the personal anecdotes and those of others that I have related regarding this faculty, have been sufficient to arouse you to investigate your own ESP abilities more fully. For while we all possess these, they are too often masked, indeed swamped, by the ordinary conscious activity of the brain, which makes their appreciation as difficult as trying to hear the chirping of a sparrow in a hedge beside which a man is operating a jack-hammer.

This is why the sages of old found it necessary to withdraw from the world and to seek out some quiet spot where they would be both free from its temptations and from its noise. There, in silent contemplation, they would listen to their inner voices and eventually make contact with, as Dionysus said, 'him who is himself above all'.

But while few of us have either the means or the desire to cut ourselves off so completely, we all have the opportunity to write down our dreams, snatch some periods of quietness wherein we may dwell within ourselves, or experiment with crystal-gazing or some other method of bringing our psychic impressions to the fore.

'Seek and ye shall find,' Jesus said. And this advice could hardly be bettered.

For the greatest mystery in the world lies within your own head. It would be a shame if you did not try to uncover some of its secrets for yourself.

And remember what the Romans said: *Hinc lucem* – From this source (we draw) light.

Index

Aberfan disaster, 76, 77
Adventure, The, 81
adyton, 95
Alexander the Great, 98-100
Ammon, oracle at, 98
animal ESP, 122-7
Anne of the Incarnation, Sister, 117
Apollo, 94-6
Asclepius, 100
Aserinsky, Eugene, 70
astral body, shape of, 132-4, 139-40
astral projection, 128-40

Barker, Dr J. C., 76
being of light, 142
Bekhterev, V. M., 122
billet reading, 149
Boswell, James, 35
Braid, James, 89
British Premonitions Bureau, 15, 16

caffeine, 40
Calchas, 66
Carington, W. Whatley, 41-2
Cassandra, 66
Chapman, Olive, quoted, 18, 35
Charon, 144
Chris, Wonder Dog, 124
clairaudience, 34, 44-9

clairsentience, 34, 49-50
clairvoyance, 9, 21-2, 25, 34-50, 124, 144
Cock Lane ghost, 103, 106
Cox boxes, 112-14
Croesus, 43-4
crystal gazing, *see* scrying

Dadashev, Tofik, 39
Dawson, Colonel, warning premonition, 73-4
de Puysegur brothers, 90
decline effect, 38-9
Dee, Dr John, 86
Delphic oracle, 94-7
dermo-optical perception, *see* eyeless-sight
dice, use of in ESP experiments, 79, 111-13
Dionysus the Areopagite, 137, 156
displacement effect, 42
divining rod, 51, 52
Dixon, Jeane, 86
Dodona, oracle at, 98
Donderi, Dr Don, 28, 29
doppelgänger, 133, 151
dowsing, 9, 51-6
dreams, 9, 67-70, 100-1, 151-3
   predictive, 67-70, 71-3

ecstasy, 116, 120
eidolon, 129
Eisenberg, Howard, 28
ethyl alcohol, 40
extra-sensory perception, 9-12, 18, 25, 44, 144
extrovert, 38
eyeless-sight, 63-5

Fanny, *see* Cock Lane ghost
Fates, Three, 93
fetch, 129
Fleming, John, 59, 60
forerunners, 74
Fox sisters, 106, 110
Freud, Sigmund, 70, 71, 100

Ganzfeld technique, 27-8, 88
Geddes, Sir Aukland, 130
Geller, Uri, 102, 103, 109
goats, 37-8, 92
Goddard, Air Marshall Sir Victor, premonitory vision of, 78-9
Goldsmith, Oliver, quoted, 103, 106
guardian spirit quest, 46, 48

Hades, 144

Hall, Asaph, 75
Harary, Keith, 135
Heaps, Dr William, 19
Herodotus, 43, 98
Hettinger, Dr J., 62
Hilprecht, Dr, 151, 152
hindsight, *see*
    retrocognition
Home, Daniel Dunglas,
    107, 120-1
Honorton, Charles, 27
Houdini, Harry, 48, 121
Houston, Jean, 90
Hurkos, Peter, 58, 61-2
hypnosis, 89-90, 92
hypnotic time distortion,
    90-2

Ibn al-Arabi, quoted,
    84-5
introvert, 38

Jephson, Ina, 26
Jesus, 103, 115-16, 156
Joan of Arc, 46
Johnson, Dr Samuel,
    quoted, 35, 36, 78
Jung, Dr Carl, 100, 128,
    129, 132

ka, 129
Kant, Immanuel, 43
Kasatkin, Dr Vasili, 100-1
Kelley, Edward, scryer,
    86
Kemensky, Yuri, 22, 28
Kulagina, Ninel, 107-8
Kuleshova, Rosa, 63-5,
    108

L-rods, 52, 53
levitation, 115-21
life after death, 10, 141-6,
    147-50
Lincoln, Abraham,
    dreams of own death,
    69
literary premonitions,
    75-6
Lombroso, Cesare, 63

Lundell, Allan, 90-2

MacGowan, Capt. A. B.,
    74
map dowsing, 52-4, 56
Maria Villani, Sister, 117
McDougall, Prof. William,
    24
medium, definition of,
    147
Messing, Wolf, 30-3, 39
Milky Bar Kid, 13-15
mini-lab, *see* Cox boxes
Moody, Dr Raymond,
    48, 141-4, 145
Moon, 40
Morris, Dr Robert, 135
Murray, Prof. Gilbert, 21,
    22
Myers, F. W. H., 34, 81

negative ions, 39
Neirhardt, Prof. John,
    112
Nero, Roman emperor,
    97
nicotine, 40
Nikolayev, Karl, 22, 28
Nirvana, 137

oak, divinatory, 98
oracles, Greek, 93-100
Origen, 146
Osty, Dr Eugene, 58-9,
    67
Otis, Dr Karlis, 134-5
out-of-body experiences,
    see astral projection

Pachomius, 115
Pearce, Hubert, 37
point of significance, 25
poltergeists, 109
positive ions, 39
Pratt, J. Gaither, 43
precognition, 9, 66-85,
    123, 153
psi-inhibitor, 38
psi-trailing, 122, 123,
    124-5

psychokinesis, 9, 79,
    102-14, 115, 121, 126
psychometry, 9, 57-65
psychoscopy, 57
Puharich, Dr Andrija,
    62, 63, 109
Pythia, Delphic priestess,
    44, 94, 95, 96

Rajah, prophetic mynah
    bird, 126-7
random event generator,
    80
REM sleep, 70
retrocognition, 9, 81-5
Rhine, Dr J. B., 23-5, 37,
    79, 111, 112, 123-4
Rhine, Louisa, 45
Robertson, Morgan, 76
Romains, Jules, 63
Ryzl, Dr Milan, 92

Schmeidler, Dr Gertrude,
    26, 37-8, 92
Schmidt, Helmut, 80
Scot, Michael, astrologer,
    85
scrying, 9, 86-9, 156
second sight, 34, 35
Sergeyev, Dr Genady,
    108
Shackleton, Basil, 42
shaman, 34
sheep, 37, 92
Sinclair, Upton, 17, 22
Soal, Dr S. G., 42
Society for Psychical
    Research, 15, 73, 150
Socrates, 46
Sperunski, Dr Sergey,
    122, 123
spiritualism, 147-50
St Joseph of Cupertino,
    115, 118-20
St Peter of Alcantara, 115
St Teresa of Avila, 116-17
Stalin, Joseph, 30, 32
Stead, William T., 75, 76
Stevenson, Ian, 20
Stewart, Gloria, 42

Sullivan, Bruce, dowser, 51, 52, 53, 54, 55
Swedenborg, Emmanuel, 43
Schweitzer, Mrs, 73

telaesthesia, 34
telekinesis, *see* psychokinesis
telepathy, 9, 17-29, 122, 123, 124, 126, 135, 144
teleportation, 114

Thouless, R. H., quoted, 102-3
Titanic sinking, 75-6
transfiguration, 154
trumpet circle, 148
Tyrell, G. N. M., quoted, 11

Venerable Bede, quoted, 145
veridical hallucination, 58, 77, 78-9

Vinogradova, Alla, 108

Ward, Billy, retrocognitive vision of, 82-84

Yellow Wolf, 47-8, 49

Zener cards, 23, 24, 25, 36-7, 79
Zener, Dr Karl, 24
Zeus, 97, 98, 99

DISCOVER ASTRAL PROJECTION	1 85538 107 9	£6.99 ☐
DISCOVER ASTROLOGY	1 85538 075 7	£7.99 ☐
DISCOVER CRYSTALS	1 85538 108 7	£7.99 ☐
DISCOVER DREAMS	1 85538 047 1	£7.99 ☐
DISCOVER GRAPHOLOGY	1 85538 059 5	£6.99 ☐
DISCOVER NUMEROLOGY	1 85538 138 9	£8.99 ☐
DISCOVER PALMISTRY	1 85538 056 0	£7.99 ☐
DISCOVER RUNES	1 85538 072 2	£6.99 ☐
DISCOVER TAROT	1 85538 048 X	£7.99 ☐

All these books are available at your local bookseller's or can be ordered direct from the publishers.

To order direct just tick the titles you want and fill in the form below:

Name: _____

Address: _____

_____

_____ Postcode: _____

Send to: Thorsons Mail Order, Dept 3J, HarperCollins*Publishers*, Westerhill Road, Bishopbriggs, Glasgow G64 2QT.
Please enclose a cheque or postal order or debit my Visa/Access account —

Credit card no: _____

Expiry date: _____

Signature: _____

— to the value of the cover price plus:
UK & BFPO: Add £1.00 for the first book and 25p for each additional book ordered.
Overseas orders including Eire: Please add £2.95 service charge. Books will be sent by surface mail but quotes for airmail despatches will be given on request.

24 HOUR TELEPHONE ORDERING SERVICE FOR ACCESS/VISA CARDHOLDERS — TEL: **041 772 2281.**